Master Long Division with Remainders Practice Workbook (Includes Examples and Answers)

Improve Your Math Fluency Series

Chris McMullen, Ph.D.

Master Long Division with Remainders Practice Workbook (Includes Examples and Answers)
Improve Your Math Fluency Series

Copyright (c) 2013 Chris McMullen, Ph.D.

All rights reserved. This includes the right to reproduce any portion of this book in any form. However, teachers who purchase one copy of this book, or borrow one physical copy from a library, may make and distribute photocopies of selected pages for instructional purposes for their own classes only. Also, parents who purchase one copy of this book, or borrow one physical copy from a library, may make and distribute photocopies of selected pages for use by their own children only.

CreateSpace

Nonfiction / Education / Elementary School
Professional & Technical / Education / Specific Skills / Mathematics
Children's / Science / Mathematics

ISBN: 1481954156

EAN-13: 978-1481954150

Master Long Division with Remainders Practice Workbook

Contents

Multiplication Table   4

Making the Most of this Workbook   5

Part 1: Practice Single-Digit Division Facts   7

Part 2: Practice Division with Single-Digit Divisors   32

Part 3: Practice Division with Double-Digit Divisors   57

Part 4: Practice Basic Remainder Problems   82

Part 5: Practice Remainders with Single-Digit Divisors   107

Part 6: Practice Multi-Digit Division with Remainders   132

Answer Key   157

Thank You

Compared to my first long division workbook, *Master Long Division Practice Workbook*, this workbook provides a page of step-by-step examples with description to help serve as a guide. There is also more workspace in four of the six chapters. I hope that you enjoy these improvements. The problems are different — so this is a new workbook, not just a new edition.

    I appreciate the suggestions for improvements and the positive comments that have been shared about the helpfulness of the Improve Your Math Fluency Series. Thank you for your interest in these workbooks. ☺

Chris McMullen

Multiplication Table

	1	2	3	4	5	6	7	8	9	10
1	1	2	3	4	5	6	7	8	9	10
2	2	4	6	8	10	12	14	16	18	20
3	3	6	9	12	15	18	21	24	27	30
4	4	8	12	16	20	24	28	32	36	40
5	5	10	15	20	25	30	35	40	45	50
6	6	12	18	24	30	36	42	48	54	60
7	7	14	21	28	35	42	49	56	63	70
8	8	16	24	32	40	48	56	64	72	80
9	9	18	27	36	45	54	63	72	81	90
10	10	20	30	40	50	60	70	80	90	100

Making the Most of this Workbook

- Mathematics is a language. You can't hold a decent conversation in any language if you have a limited vocabulary or if you are not fluent. In order to become successful in mathematics, you need to practice until you have mastered the fundamentals and developed fluency in the subject. This *Master Long Division with Remainders Practice Workbook* will help you improve your long division skills.

- You may need to consult the multiplication table on page 4 occasionally as you begin your practice, but should refrain from relying on it. Force yourself to solve the problems independently as much as possible. It is necessary to memorize the basic multiplication facts and know them quickly in order to become successful at long division.

- Use Part 1 of this book to improve your proficiency with fundamental division facts that have single-digit divisors and quotients. Fluency with these fundamentals is critical toward mastering long division.

- Part 2 of this book is limited to single-digit divisors without remainders. This way you are not challenged with too much at once.

- Double-digit divisors are the focus of Part 3, which still does not have remainders.

- Remainders are introduced in Part 4, beginning with single-digit divisors.

- The dividends become larger in Part 5, which still has single-digit divisors and remainders.

- Part 6 of this book includes a variety of multi-digit division problems which have remainders. You are ready to move onto Part 6 when you can complete the practice pages of Parts 2 thru 5 quickly with few mistakes. Part 6 will help you develop proficiency in long division.

- A couple of step-by-step examples with description are included to help serve as a guide.

- After you complete a page, check your answers at the back of the book. Practice makes permanent, but not necessarily perfect: If you practice making mistakes, you will learn your mistakes. Check your answers and learn from your mistakes such that you practice solving the problems correctly. This way your practice will make perfect.

- Math can be fun. Make a game of your practice by recording your times and trying to improve on your times, and recording your scores and trying to improve on your scores. Doing this will help you see how much you are improving, and this sign of improvement can give you the confidence to succeed in math, which can help you learn to enjoy this subject more.

Master Long Division with Remainders Practice Workbook

Part 1: Practice Single-Digit Division Facts

Division facts: This first chapter provides plenty of practice with the fundamental single-digit division facts between the numbers 1 and 81. It is invaluable to become fluent in your division facts before moving onto long division.

Definitions: The **dividend** is divided by the **divisor** and the result of the division is called the **quotient**. For example, in 24 ÷ 4 = 6, 24 is the dividend and 4 is the divisor, while 6 is their quotient.

Multiplication table: A multiplication table is included on page 4 for students who are still learning (or have forgotten some of) their multiplication and division facts. Here is how the multiplication table works: Find the divisor in the left column and the dividend in the same row as the divisor; the quotient will appear in the top row directly above the dividend. Put another way, the row of the divisor and the column of the quotient intersect at the dividend. It may be simpler to understand this visually by comparing the following examples with the multiplication table on page 4.

Examples:

$3 \overline{) 18}$ = 6   Look at the left column and find the 3. Go across 3's row to find the 18. Find the number in the top row directly above the 18. This is 6.

$5 \overline{) 20}$ = 4   Look at the left column and find the 5. Go across 5's row to find the 20. Find the number in the top row directly above the 20. This is 4.

Note: Division facts are easy if you know your multiplication facts. For example, if you know that 4 × 6 = 24, it's easy to figure out that 24 ÷ 4 = 6 or 24 ÷ 6 = 4.

Independence: You may need to use the multiplication table when you first start using this workbook, but you should strive to remember the division facts. Your goal is to be able to correctly write the answers without looking at the multiplication table.

Practice: Practice the exercises in this chapter until you are fluent in your division facts.

Time/score: Time yourself using a stopwatch. When you complete the page, record your time at the top of the page. Check your answers in the back of the book, and record your score at the top of the page. This way, you can see how much you are improving on your prior performance.

Mastery: Once you are fluent in your division facts, you are ready to move onto the next chapter.

Improve Your Math Fluency Series

Time: _____   Score: _____

8)48	6)42	1)2	5)40	9)54	1)4
2)4	6)42	7)21	1)7	7)21	7)14
8)16	4)4	9)54	8)48	2)18	4)28
4)16	7)21	5)5	6)42	4)36	2)12
2)16	1)1	5)5	9)36	5)5	4)16
9)63	5)25	7)63	8)8	5)20	5)25
7)14	2)10	6)12	9)9	6)18	4)16
6)18	8)72	9)27	2)8	5)10	4)4
3)3	9)18	1)5	2)10	6)30	2)16
5)15	3)21	6)24	6)48	1)8	5)30
6)48	4)20	9)54	9)18	4)12	8)16
3)24	5)15	7)7	8)64	1)5	4)32

Master Long Division with Remainders Practice Workbook

Time: _____   Score: _____

$3\overline{)9}$	$5\overline{)30}$	$3\overline{)27}$	$5\overline{)40}$	$1\overline{)1}$	$3\overline{)24}$
$8\overline{)40}$	$2\overline{)14}$	$9\overline{)9}$	$8\overline{)56}$	$2\overline{)6}$	$8\overline{)64}$
$5\overline{)10}$	$8\overline{)16}$	$5\overline{)5}$	$1\overline{)4}$	$4\overline{)32}$	$9\overline{)27}$
$6\overline{)24}$	$1\overline{)4}$	$9\overline{)63}$	$1\overline{)1}$	$6\overline{)42}$	$4\overline{)16}$
$9\overline{)18}$	$5\overline{)20}$	$8\overline{)32}$	$3\overline{)3}$	$6\overline{)42}$	$6\overline{)30}$
$3\overline{)27}$	$9\overline{)18}$	$9\overline{)81}$	$9\overline{)45}$	$3\overline{)6}$	$8\overline{)24}$
$2\overline{)10}$	$7\overline{)63}$	$8\overline{)32}$	$7\overline{)42}$	$7\overline{)49}$	$9\overline{)27}$
$3\overline{)15}$	$5\overline{)15}$	$8\overline{)32}$	$9\overline{)81}$	$7\overline{)49}$	$3\overline{)24}$
$5\overline{)15}$	$2\overline{)8}$	$8\overline{)16}$	$6\overline{)54}$	$8\overline{)40}$	$9\overline{)36}$
$2\overline{)4}$	$9\overline{)45}$	$2\overline{)4}$	$6\overline{)12}$	$6\overline{)12}$	$8\overline{)32}$
$6\overline{)42}$	$9\overline{)9}$	$2\overline{)18}$	$3\overline{)6}$	$2\overline{)8}$	$1\overline{)8}$
$5\overline{)40}$	$2\overline{)4}$	$5\overline{)25}$	$8\overline{)8}$	$5\overline{)45}$	$3\overline{)6}$

Improve Your Math Fluency Series

Time: _____   Score: _____

4)20	6)36	1)9	8)16	4)4	4)16
4)4	1)9	1)8	1)4	7)56	2)18
1)5	4)16	6)12	5)25	1)2	1)5
3)15	2)8	6)30	3)12	4)24	3)9
1)2	7)35	3)15	7)21	5)45	6)24
9)9	6)18	6)6	1)5	5)40	7)14
1)4	3)15	1)7	7)35	8)16	5)35
3)18	5)35	7)63	6)36	9)54	9)45
3)6	7)7	7)35	7)49	2)2	1)6
4)24	4)12	9)27	6)54	5)20	1)9
7)35	8)32	5)40	4)28	9)9	2)4
7)42	1)5	3)24	8)16	5)25	7)35

Master Long Division with Remainders Practice Workbook

Time: _____ Score: _____

8)24	1)4	4)4	8)56	3)12	2)18
5)25	9)54	7)28	4)16	2)16	2)10
2)10	2)18	6)24	3)15	3)9	3)3
5)40	3)27	9)63	4)16	8)40	9)36
6)48	9)18	6)18	6)54	9)27	6)36
2)10	6)18	8)16	4)12	1)2	7)28
1)2	6)30	3)24	3)15	7)56	2)12
8)16	7)63	1)1	7)42	6)42	7)14
2)2	9)9	8)16	2)8	7)21	5)40
6)36	5)40	6)24	8)24	6)12	3)9
6)36	7)14	4)4	1)6	8)72	6)6
9)72	9)54	9)9	3)3	8)16	3)3

11

Improve Your Math Fluency Series

Time: _____   Score: _____

8)56	7)42	7)14	8)48	8)56	6)12
2)10	3)12	1)3	3)27	1)4	5)45
1)2	7)63	2)8	2)10	8)8	2)4
8)32	9)54	3)24	8)24	3)27	5)5
1)4	9)36	2)14	4)28	1)3	4)8
7)14	9)27	5)25	6)42	5)40	9)54
6)48	1)6	3)6	5)45	9)36	3)21
7)42	4)32	4)36	2)14	7)42	2)4
2)2	5)5	6)6	6)6	4)20	7)21
2)6	1)5	3)9	4)12	2)8	8)56
6)42	2)14	8)72	2)4	7)21	1)1
5)30	2)2	7)28	4)24	1)6	3)27

Master Long Division with Remainders Practice Workbook

Time: _____   Score: _____

$6\overline{)6}$	$6\overline{)54}$	$5\overline{)35}$	$9\overline{)9}$	$5\overline{)25}$	$8\overline{)16}$
$7\overline{)35}$	$1\overline{)9}$	$7\overline{)21}$	$2\overline{)2}$	$4\overline{)36}$	$9\overline{)81}$
$4\overline{)12}$	$4\overline{)28}$	$1\overline{)7}$	$4\overline{)28}$	$5\overline{)45}$	$4\overline{)24}$
$1\overline{)7}$	$2\overline{)12}$	$1\overline{)3}$	$5\overline{)5}$	$1\overline{)4}$	$9\overline{)63}$
$7\overline{)28}$	$1\overline{)8}$	$8\overline{)16}$	$7\overline{)7}$	$8\overline{)48}$	$3\overline{)9}$
$9\overline{)18}$	$1\overline{)9}$	$2\overline{)10}$	$4\overline{)20}$	$6\overline{)36}$	$2\overline{)6}$
$3\overline{)27}$	$4\overline{)20}$	$5\overline{)45}$	$3\overline{)9}$	$9\overline{)72}$	$9\overline{)72}$
$4\overline{)24}$	$2\overline{)6}$	$6\overline{)36}$	$4\overline{)12}$	$2\overline{)10}$	$3\overline{)6}$
$4\overline{)36}$	$8\overline{)48}$	$3\overline{)18}$	$6\overline{)12}$	$4\overline{)28}$	$5\overline{)30}$
$1\overline{)7}$	$1\overline{)5}$	$3\overline{)24}$	$8\overline{)64}$	$3\overline{)3}$	$3\overline{)24}$
$4\overline{)4}$	$3\overline{)6}$	$4\overline{)24}$	$5\overline{)40}$	$9\overline{)18}$	$6\overline{)54}$
$8\overline{)56}$	$9\overline{)72}$	$3\overline{)27}$	$5\overline{)40}$	$6\overline{)42}$	$8\overline{)56}$

Improve Your Math Fluency Series

Time: _____   Score: _____

$7\overline{)35}$	$3\overline{)24}$	$6\overline{)54}$	$2\overline{)6}$	$3\overline{)18}$	$4\overline{)20}$
$5\overline{)15}$	$5\overline{)5}$	$8\overline{)72}$	$4\overline{)8}$	$8\overline{)72}$	$4\overline{)28}$
$9\overline{)45}$	$4\overline{)32}$	$9\overline{)81}$	$6\overline{)42}$	$4\overline{)32}$	$4\overline{)24}$
$6\overline{)36}$	$4\overline{)4}$	$2\overline{)4}$	$3\overline{)27}$	$5\overline{)20}$	$2\overline{)14}$
$7\overline{)7}$	$9\overline{)9}$	$2\overline{)4}$	$7\overline{)63}$	$9\overline{)45}$	$7\overline{)21}$
$9\overline{)27}$	$9\overline{)54}$	$6\overline{)36}$	$6\overline{)12}$	$7\overline{)63}$	$7\overline{)35}$
$3\overline{)9}$	$1\overline{)5}$	$4\overline{)12}$	$8\overline{)8}$	$4\overline{)8}$	$5\overline{)25}$
$5\overline{)25}$	$3\overline{)3}$	$6\overline{)36}$	$8\overline{)40}$	$9\overline{)45}$	$1\overline{)1}$
$1\overline{)1}$	$6\overline{)36}$	$4\overline{)16}$	$6\overline{)36}$	$7\overline{)7}$	$5\overline{)10}$
$5\overline{)20}$	$5\overline{)30}$	$8\overline{)32}$	$8\overline{)56}$	$5\overline{)45}$	$3\overline{)6}$
$8\overline{)40}$	$7\overline{)7}$	$9\overline{)36}$	$1\overline{)2}$	$5\overline{)5}$	$6\overline{)48}$
$9\overline{)45}$	$3\overline{)27}$	$6\overline{)12}$	$2\overline{)10}$	$9\overline{)18}$	$2\overline{)12}$

Master Long Division with Remainders Practice Workbook

Time: _____   Score: _____

9)̄72	8)̄24	1)̄5	9)̄36	3)̄21	7)̄21
5)̄25	8)̄8	3)̄21	8)̄40	7)̄14	3)̄21
4)̄28	5)̄25	9)̄9	4)̄4	2)̄6	9)̄36
9)̄27	9)̄18	8)̄48	8)̄72	4)̄36	7)̄56
3)̄15	4)̄36	9)̄18	7)̄28	6)̄18	3)̄12
2)̄10	7)̄56	1)̄9	9)̄9	5)̄30	6)̄36
9)̄81	1)̄8	8)̄16	6)̄24	9)̄54	8)̄64
1)̄4	8)̄16	5)̄15	9)̄9	4)̄16	4)̄32
1)̄6	9)̄54	1)̄1	4)̄28	9)̄9	4)̄16
7)̄14	1)̄2	6)̄24	5)̄5	4)̄20	3)̄27
5)̄35	6)̄36	6)̄36	8)̄64	9)̄27	7)̄63
4)̄20	5)̄20	4)̄12	2)̄6	9)̄45	1)̄4

Improve Your Math Fluency Series

Time: _____   Score: _____

2)6	7)14	7)56	7)49	8)56	9)9
3)12	2)16	3)18	2)4	5)5	6)24
8)72	1)3	6)12	8)56	3)9	9)72
8)56	6)42	1)8	3)15	8)40	1)8
5)5	9)63	3)24	2)6	2)10	9)9
4)16	7)56	9)36	2)4	2)8	5)5
2)2	4)28	5)10	9)9	5)30	3)12
1)2	2)2	2)6	4)4	6)36	3)21
3)6	5)30	9)18	7)7	6)30	3)21
3)6	5)10	3)9	1)6	4)20	6)36
7)56	8)56	7)14	7)14	5)35	4)20
5)20	6)54	9)54	1)7	6)36	5)45

Master Long Division with Remainders Practice Workbook

Time: _____   Score: _____

9)54	1)2	7)49	3)6	4)12	4)16
2)10	1)1	1)2	8)48	4)32	9)9
5)25	8)56	7)49	1)2	7)56	3)15
2)14	4)36	9)54	4)36	7)14	9)54
4)32	9)18	6)42	8)32	2)10	4)36
7)7	7)14	9)63	9)45	4)36	5)20
1)7	9)18	2)12	5)10	3)6	9)63
3)21	1)4	4)28	7)35	9)45	1)5
6)6	8)8	1)3	3)21	7)63	2)14
3)12	2)8	4)16	3)24	1)6	1)3
9)72	7)42	3)21	5)25	8)24	8)24
4)28	8)16	4)4	5)45	4)16	9)9

Improve Your Math Fluency Series

Time: _____   Score: _____

$4\overline{)24}$	$8\overline{)8}$	$3\overline{)27}$	$3\overline{)12}$	$1\overline{)6}$	$4\overline{)24}$
$1\overline{)8}$	$1\overline{)9}$	$1\overline{)8}$	$1\overline{)6}$	$7\overline{)49}$	$9\overline{)36}$
$2\overline{)18}$	$4\overline{)8}$	$1\overline{)3}$	$3\overline{)27}$	$4\overline{)12}$	$6\overline{)42}$
$9\overline{)72}$	$9\overline{)45}$	$6\overline{)30}$	$8\overline{)72}$	$1\overline{)7}$	$3\overline{)15}$
$4\overline{)20}$	$3\overline{)12}$	$5\overline{)45}$	$4\overline{)12}$	$6\overline{)54}$	$7\overline{)7}$
$1\overline{)1}$	$9\overline{)45}$	$2\overline{)12}$	$7\overline{)14}$	$9\overline{)27}$	$4\overline{)8}$
$7\overline{)7}$	$5\overline{)40}$	$2\overline{)14}$	$9\overline{)45}$	$4\overline{)16}$	$2\overline{)12}$
$3\overline{)6}$	$2\overline{)16}$	$2\overline{)10}$	$4\overline{)28}$	$2\overline{)8}$	$3\overline{)27}$
$7\overline{)21}$	$5\overline{)15}$	$9\overline{)18}$	$1\overline{)2}$	$6\overline{)6}$	$3\overline{)18}$
$6\overline{)54}$	$9\overline{)27}$	$1\overline{)3}$	$4\overline{)12}$	$8\overline{)40}$	$5\overline{)35}$
$8\overline{)24}$	$9\overline{)36}$	$1\overline{)5}$	$9\overline{)81}$	$6\overline{)12}$	$3\overline{)12}$
$1\overline{)3}$	$1\overline{)1}$	$8\overline{)64}$	$1\overline{)6}$	$1\overline{)3}$	$1\overline{)6}$

Master Long Division with Remainders Practice Workbook

Time: _____   Score: _____

8)56	8)24	7)14	7)7	6)30	2)8
1)5	5)40	1)2	2)14	4)28	3)21
2)6	8)72	6)12	6)42	3)24	1)5
9)54	2)2	7)42	8)32	1)2	9)72
6)36	9)27	6)6	5)20	2)2	7)56
5)45	1)5	4)16	5)45	3)9	7)7
3)27	2)8	7)63	8)16	4)32	9)81
3)24	5)35	3)15	5)20	1)9	5)10
3)12	9)54	2)16	3)24	8)24	4)12
5)25	7)56	1)1	4)4	6)12	1)7
9)63	6)18	5)45	1)1	5)45	5)30
1)6	9)54	5)45	3)21	2)18	5)20

19

Improve Your Math Fluency Series

Time: _____   Score: _____

1)2   1)3   1)3   6)48   3)12   4)36

8)32   1)4   7)42   2)8   7)63   1)1

7)28   1)8   6)12   5)5   6)54   2)4

8)24   7)7   1)6   5)35   7)35   4)12

7)28   8)72   7)14   3)15   3)24   4)28

7)35   7)49   8)8   9)63   6)18   8)72

2)10   5)25   9)54   5)10   5)15   6)24

2)2   5)45   9)45   7)56   8)72   5)45

2)2   5)15   3)24   7)63   9)45   2)10

5)40   7)28   4)24   3)18   3)27   5)10

5)45   1)6   5)10   5)5   1)7   4)4

2)4   2)8   6)36   4)24   2)16   1)8

Master Long Division with Remainders Practice Workbook

Time: _____ Score: _____

$3\overline{)27}$	$7\overline{)35}$	$2\overline{)6}$	$9\overline{)18}$	$4\overline{)8}$	$7\overline{)21}$
$5\overline{)30}$	$8\overline{)32}$	$9\overline{)18}$	$7\overline{)63}$	$6\overline{)36}$	$2\overline{)14}$
$9\overline{)63}$	$4\overline{)12}$	$7\overline{)21}$	$2\overline{)14}$	$7\overline{)28}$	$2\overline{)12}$
$8\overline{)40}$	$8\overline{)40}$	$3\overline{)15}$	$3\overline{)12}$	$9\overline{)18}$	$3\overline{)27}$
$4\overline{)4}$	$7\overline{)63}$	$6\overline{)42}$	$3\overline{)27}$	$4\overline{)24}$	$7\overline{)63}$
$2\overline{)6}$	$2\overline{)12}$	$8\overline{)48}$	$7\overline{)56}$	$9\overline{)36}$	$5\overline{)45}$
$9\overline{)36}$	$1\overline{)7}$	$4\overline{)16}$	$3\overline{)6}$	$7\overline{)42}$	$8\overline{)56}$
$8\overline{)64}$	$9\overline{)45}$	$1\overline{)3}$	$7\overline{)63}$	$6\overline{)6}$	$8\overline{)56}$
$4\overline{)28}$	$8\overline{)56}$	$8\overline{)32}$	$7\overline{)14}$	$7\overline{)35}$	$6\overline{)42}$
$8\overline{)24}$	$5\overline{)15}$	$2\overline{)2}$	$5\overline{)10}$	$3\overline{)3}$	$2\overline{)18}$
$5\overline{)40}$	$5\overline{)10}$	$8\overline{)48}$	$5\overline{)10}$	$4\overline{)20}$	$8\overline{)32}$
$6\overline{)12}$	$5\overline{)45}$	$1\overline{)5}$	$1\overline{)4}$	$8\overline{)40}$	$2\overline{)4}$

Improve Your Math Fluency Series

Time: _____   Score: _____

8)32	4)36	2)16	4)16	4)16	7)56
7)21	1)6	6)18	8)16	5)45	7)28
3)27	6)54	7)28	2)12	7)42	5)15
4)12	5)30	1)5	6)30	9)18	6)42
3)27	4)8	9)18	7)7	1)8	3)3
4)32	3)27	3)12	5)45	7)56	4)24
7)35	5)35	7)42	7)42	8)48	5)25
1)9	6)48	7)14	3)27	9)27	2)4
5)45	9)9	7)49	7)28	1)8	9)63
4)32	8)16	8)56	5)25	3)24	9)45
4)16	1)1	3)18	3)24	4)28	1)4
1)6	1)6	9)27	7)35	9)45	6)24

Master Long Division with Remainders Practice Workbook

Time: _____   Score: _____

6)54	2)10	1)2	9)18	8)32	2)6
1)4	7)21	2)2	3)15	2)18	1)3
8)32	8)64	4)24	1)6	5)5	5)30
2)2	7)56	9)72	3)27	1)6	4)12
8)48	2)14	7)21	7)56	4)24	8)16
6)48	4)20	7)21	1)2	2)12	9)9
7)7	4)4	5)20	5)10	4)36	8)32
7)21	5)10	4)12	4)16	9)36	3)15
6)36	5)25	4)28	9)45	7)35	3)27
7)28	8)40	2)12	4)24	5)10	5)5
6)18	2)16	5)10	5)15	6)48	9)9
2)14	2)10	4)8	6)54	4)20	7)63

Improve Your Math Fluency Series

Time: _____   Score: _____

7)21	8)32	2)10	9)63	9)36	5)20
5)35	2)16	7)42	8)16	8)16	3)27
1)2	6)30	2)10	3)15	6)42	2)8
8)56	7)49	6)6	7)28	6)30	4)32
7)7	4)32	2)8	4)32	5)10	8)64
6)42	6)30	3)12	5)45	7)42	5)25
5)45	2)10	9)9	5)45	8)40	9)9
3)9	9)72	8)48	7)28	4)12	1)6
9)63	7)7	9)9	8)40	3)18	1)2
5)5	3)3	6)18	5)20	7)35	5)40
8)40	3)21	3)27	7)42	2)6	6)12
9)63	4)24	7)49	6)12	1)9	8)16

Master Long Division with Remainders Practice Workbook

Time: _____   Score: _____

1)8	6)18	5)5	8)40	2)4	2)2
7)56	4)20	6)48	8)40	9)63	4)8
2)8	8)56	8)48	5)45	3)9	6)48
6)54	3)6	8)24	3)27	3)27	7)42
8)72	1)3	2)18	9)72	9)27	1)8
7)42	2)18	6)36	5)5	6)18	8)16
4)12	5)35	5)20	8)40	3)3	5)5
8)32	2)2	7)63	4)12	4)4	8)40
3)3	5)5	2)12	9)72	6)12	7)49
9)36	3)15	9)81	9)45	2)2	4)24
8)48	5)5	5)20	5)10	7)63	4)32
3)27	8)72	9)9	2)2	2)18	1)1

Improve Your Math Fluency Series

Time: _____   Score: _____

1)7	2)8	4)8	5)25	9)36	2)16
9)81	8)72	3)9	5)10	5)35	9)81
9)36	3)27	5)35	7)7	9)45	2)8
3)18	9)72	1)5	6)42	6)36	4)4
9)27	6)30	3)15	8)8	5)40	2)8
9)36	1)2	9)27	9)45	3)6	8)16
2)8	3)27	1)6	9)27	7)63	1)6
3)3	4)28	3)12	7)63	8)8	6)54
3)9	6)18	6)30	6)6	2)10	5)35
8)24	4)8	1)3	1)8	5)15	7)21
3)15	4)36	3)21	5)20	6)18	9)63
1)6	1)5	8)32	6)36	7)35	6)48

Master Long Division with Remainders Practice Workbook

Time: _____   Score: _____

3)6	8)24	9)45	3)3	5)40	5)30
4)28	7)21	4)28	9)36	8)32	3)27
9)81	7)49	7)56	2)16	9)45	7)35
7)56	3)27	4)32	4)4	5)5	9)27
9)45	9)72	2)2	3)24	5)15	5)30
5)15	2)16	6)18	5)45	4)36	5)5
9)9	6)36	7)35	3)24	1)5	8)16
8)40	8)48	9)45	4)8	4)28	8)24
6)36	7)7	7)14	3)21	1)6	1)2
4)8	3)24	3)9	8)72	4)36	5)15
1)3	1)7	6)18	8)16	8)32	5)25
7)63	1)6	9)27	3)12	3)27	1)4

27

Improve Your Math Fluency Series

Time: _____   Score: _____

8)24	3)12	2)16	1)4	9)81	8)24
3)21	5)30	6)54	1)9	3)9	4)36
9)54	5)15	6)42	6)48	1)7	3)15
6)54	7)35	5)25	1)7	1)4	7)63
1)2	4)28	4)16	1)6	7)21	5)40
5)20	2)12	3)24	4)24	2)8	1)6
7)63	8)56	2)10	3)18	5)15	3)18
7)7	1)5	7)14	8)32	8)8	9)72
9)9	2)18	9)27	2)12	3)9	4)24
8)40	1)2	3)27	1)7	3)27	3)21
8)24	9)54	5)25	7)56	9)18	9)81
3)9	2)12	4)8	4)32	8)48	4)20

Master Long Division with Remainders Practice Workbook

Time: _____   Score: _____

4)16	6)54	1)6	8)8	7)56	8)24
1)2	5)45	2)10	8)56	1)8	5)10
5)10	5)25	2)8	9)18	2)12	5)45
6)18	4)8	4)24	1)5	3)6	2)8
9)63	6)24	8)16	6)24	3)9	6)54
3)3	3)21	8)72	2)4	8)56	8)64
8)56	5)10	3)9	6)42	1)5	2)16
6)12	2)14	8)40	1)8	1)2	1)4
9)18	8)48	2)18	6)54	8)56	1)3
9)36	4)28	3)9	1)3	7)28	1)9
4)16	4)24	4)24	1)8	4)8	1)4
3)15	9)63	9)45	7)49	7)42	2)14

Improve Your Math Fluency Series

Time: _____   Score: _____

$9\overline{)36}$	$8\overline{)64}$	$3\overline{)6}$	$2\overline{)16}$	$7\overline{)28}$	$7\overline{)35}$
$2\overline{)6}$	$3\overline{)21}$	$6\overline{)42}$	$6\overline{)48}$	$9\overline{)45}$	$2\overline{)12}$
$8\overline{)48}$	$9\overline{)63}$	$6\overline{)48}$	$9\overline{)18}$	$9\overline{)18}$	$4\overline{)16}$
$8\overline{)56}$	$7\overline{)28}$	$3\overline{)24}$	$3\overline{)21}$	$8\overline{)16}$	$1\overline{)4}$
$2\overline{)4}$	$6\overline{)24}$	$1\overline{)2}$	$4\overline{)28}$	$5\overline{)20}$	$1\overline{)3}$
$7\overline{)56}$	$1\overline{)9}$	$7\overline{)56}$	$9\overline{)81}$	$5\overline{)5}$	$4\overline{)36}$
$5\overline{)15}$	$8\overline{)64}$	$9\overline{)45}$	$2\overline{)10}$	$3\overline{)12}$	$9\overline{)18}$
$2\overline{)4}$	$9\overline{)63}$	$2\overline{)18}$	$5\overline{)20}$	$6\overline{)30}$	$1\overline{)5}$
$6\overline{)42}$	$7\overline{)21}$	$2\overline{)6}$	$9\overline{)72}$	$3\overline{)3}$	$1\overline{)6}$
$6\overline{)42}$	$4\overline{)12}$	$6\overline{)12}$	$1\overline{)8}$	$8\overline{)72}$	$8\overline{)32}$
$8\overline{)16}$	$9\overline{)27}$	$3\overline{)15}$	$6\overline{)24}$	$1\overline{)1}$	$1\overline{)5}$
$9\overline{)81}$	$2\overline{)10}$	$9\overline{)72}$	$7\overline{)49}$	$1\overline{)5}$	$8\overline{)72}$

Master Long Division with Remainders Practice Workbook

Time: _____   Score: _____

7)28	2)4	8)72	5)25	2)2	2)8
3)21	5)15	6)6	5)35	7)14	7)63
1)6	3)15	8)8	3)12	9)9	7)21
4)24	2)4	1)6	3)24	3)24	9)36
6)12	4)20	9)18	5)15	4)20	7)63
3)9	5)15	4)32	9)63	7)42	2)6
9)63	7)63	7)14	9)81	7)42	4)8
2)6	5)45	7)35	8)72	3)21	8)32
5)5	1)9	8)72	4)20	7)42	2)6
5)15	8)48	5)10	3)21	5)30	6)24
1)9	4)12	6)18	6)42	6)6	3)21
6)24	3)12	6)42	3)12	1)1	5)45

Part 2: Practice Division with Single-Digit Divisors

Single-digit divisors: In this chapter, the dividend has up to 4 digits while the divisor is a single-digit number.

Step-by-step examples:

❶ The 5 doesn't go into 2, so don't write a number above the 2 of 215. ❷ Look at 21 instead of 2. ❸ The largest number 5 can make that doesn't exceed 21 is 20. ❹ Write 20 below 21. ❺ Since 5 times 4 equals 20, write a 4 above the 1 of 215. ❻ Subtract 20 from 21 to make 1. ❼ Bring down the 5 to make 15. ❽ Next, 5 divides evenly into 15. ❾ Write 15 below 15. ❿ Since 5 times 3 equals 15, write a 3 above the 5 of 215. ⓫ Subtract 15 from 15 to make 0.

❶ The largest number 3 can make that doesn't exceed 8 is 6. ❷ Write 6 below 8. ❸ Since 3 times 2 equals 6, write a 2 above the 8 of 8124. ❹ Subtract 6 from 8 to make 2. ❺ Bring down the 1 to make 21. ❻ Next, 3 divides evenly into 21. ❼ Write 21 below 21. ❽ Since 3 times 7 equals 21, write a 7 above the 1 of 8124. ❾ Since 21 minus 21 equals 0, bring down the 2. ❿ Because 3 doesn't go into 2, write a 0 above the 2 of 8124. ⓫ Bring down the 4 to make 24. ⓬ Next, 3 divides evenly into 24. ⓭ Write 24 below 24. ⓮ Since 3 times 8 equals 24, write an 8 above the 4 of 8124. ⓯ Subtract 24 from 24 to make 0.

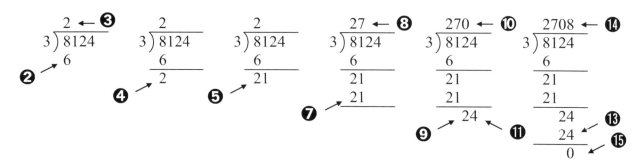

Guide: Refer to the examples above and use them as a guide. Check your answers to make sure that you are practicing correctly. Once you get the hang of it, try to solve the problems without looking at the examples. Practice this chapter until you become fluent.

Master Long Division with Remainders Practice Workbook

Time: _____ Score: _____

6)216   8)448   5)1170   4)40   7)1274

5)1555   6)60   3)81   7)854   2)84

7)2828   3)1368   7)3885   7)427   8)96

Improve Your Math Fluency Series

Time: _____   Score: _____

8)432   8)4008   4)76   9)3924   3)792

4)296   6)444   3)1461   4)280   3)1365

8)6992   4)2612   6)5454   3)276   4)384

Master Long Division with Remainders Practice Workbook

Time: _____   Score: _____

2) 1916   2) 64   2) 466   5) 1185   2) 586

7) 5194   6) 2868   6) 1968   6) 4398   5) 475

3) 108   5) 4290   6) 252   8) 7200   8) 80

Improve Your Math Fluency Series

Time: _____   Score: _____

2) 132   8) 712   3) 543   8) 552   2) 362

7) 616   6) 462   6) 378   8) 336   5) 3420

2) 1414   4) 1764   7) 1302   3) 1947   9) 108

Master Long Division with Remainders Practice Workbook

Time: _____ Score: _____

3) 1113   6) 882   6) 486   2) 92   4) 1968

6) 258   4) 1612   7) 2219   7) 798   4) 80

9) 774   7) 98   4) 1136   3) 2388   8) 232

Improve Your Math Fluency Series

Time: _____   Score: _____

6) 582   9) 612   7) 553   9) 468   6) 570

2) 1326   7) 5348   8) 288   9) 6435   3) 231

3) 105   3) 45   5) 160   3) 33   5) 410

Master Long Division with Remainders Practice Workbook

Time: _____   Score: _____

5) 4860   3) 2688   3) 2130   2) 120   6) 408

2) 1388   9) 864   6) 4962   8) 3576   5) 870

8) 688   4) 168   5) 1055   5) 235   4) 156

Improve Your Math Fluency Series

Time: _____   Score: _____

2) 32   3) 1416   7) 4984   3) 84   7) 6755

4) 340   3) 1590   2) 94   9) 4023   5) 4145

9) 261   4) 384   2) 826   8) 2440   9) 108

Master Long Division with Remainders Practice Workbook

Time: _____   Score: _____

8) 7920   9) 1710   9) 441   3) 231   9) 1188

6) 156   3) 2817   6) 2220   2) 100   9) 6813

5) 4845   7) 6608   7) 98   4) 104   9) 1611

Improve Your Math Fluency Series

Time: _____   Score: _____

6) 270   5) 1870   9) 387   4) 968   3) 267

6) 4536   4) 484   6) 1386   6) 246   4) 108

5) 4395   8) 5184   7) 4340   8) 384   2) 1932

Master Long Division with Remainders Practice Workbook

Time: _____   Score: _____

4) 192   8) 6200   9) 8460   2) 220   8) 264

9) 8838   3) 537   5) 2935   8) 536   6) 270

6) 1140   4) 636   3) 168   3) 225   8) 784

Improve Your Math Fluency Series

Time: _____   Score: _____

6) 456   9) 891   5) 4925   3) 186   9) 5121

7) 546   2) 1250   3) 2688   4) 992   9) 5580

6) 1422   2) 82   3) 255   5) 4365   4) 3828

Master Long Division with Remainders Practice Workbook

Time: _____   Score: _____

7) 371   3) 288   6) 5106   9) 864   3) 192

8) 664   8) 160   2) 118   8) 6344   3) 291

7) 665   7) 3003   3) 525   4) 296   5) 335

Improve Your Math Fluency Series

Time: _____   Score: _____

4) 504   3) 168   7) 4158   2) 1132   7) 1267

6) 696   3) 129   9) 198   5) 1590   5) 420

7) 5565   7) 238   6) 186   2) 1134   6) 5814

Master Long Division with Remainders Practice Workbook

Time: _____ Score: _____

$8\overline{)4200}$ $6\overline{)2244}$ $8\overline{)776}$ $7\overline{)5446}$ $3\overline{)1137}$

$6\overline{)1332}$ $3\overline{)111}$ $7\overline{)4648}$ $4\overline{)1808}$ $3\overline{)180}$

$6\overline{)3606}$ $9\overline{)6291}$ $5\overline{)170}$ $2\overline{)500}$ $7\overline{)203}$

Improve Your Math Fluency Series

Time: _____ Score: _____

7)511   2)1916   3)237   6)3660   8)6880

8)6544   3)2406   4)392   6)162   2)206

6)1032   7)637   2)94   5)185   6)408

Master Long Division with Remainders Practice Workbook

Time: _____ Score: _____

2) 58   8) 176   7) 490   4) 2364   2) 62

2) 24   6) 336   4) 2028   4) 144   8) 3552

9) 675   3) 2832   4) 2604   6) 1770   9) 2529

Improve Your Math Fluency Series

Time: _____   Score: _____

$2 \overline{)70}$ $2 \overline{)770}$ $3 \overline{)2238}$ $2 \overline{)1800}$ $2 \overline{)1112}$

$3 \overline{)354}$ $3 \overline{)1257}$ $3 \overline{)204}$ $5 \overline{)340}$ $7 \overline{)4452}$

$2 \overline{)96}$ $7 \overline{)4473}$ $6 \overline{)4566}$ $6 \overline{)5916}$ $7 \overline{)4977}$

Master Long Division with Remainders Practice Workbook

Time: _____   Score: _____

2) 1024   4) 984   8) 7568   3) 72   5) 3630

2) 176   5) 440   7) 1400   9) 513   6) 528

2) 1732   8) 3768   3) 384   5) 3210   8) 296

Improve Your Math Fluency Series

Time: _____   Score: _____

$7\overline{)826}$ $7\overline{)5579}$ $3\overline{)276}$ $8\overline{)2888}$ $2\overline{)152}$

$6\overline{)918}$ $7\overline{)644}$ $4\overline{)2940}$ $9\overline{)3519}$ $2\overline{)100}$

$6\overline{)5388}$ $2\overline{)88}$ $7\overline{)3703}$ $6\overline{)66}$ $8\overline{)3368}$

Master Long Division with Remainders Practice Workbook

Time: _____   Score: _____

6) 84   9) 1296   4) 2724   3) 2292   4) 1092

3) 135   3) 1314   7) 5516   6) 528   4) 1188

8) 2456   9) 8757   5) 1550   7) 679   3) 183

Improve Your Math Fluency Series

Time: _____   Score: _____

4) 1156   3) 180   8) 1128   2) 114   5) 2860

9) 3213   8) 696   8) 1560   5) 2340   3) 2850

6) 1530   9) 414   9) 1917   5) 80   8) 560

Master Long Division with Remainders Practice Workbook

Time: _____ Score: _____

3) 126   7) 553   2) 1004   8) 792   7) 476

8) 3480   9) 891   4) 368   5) 190   9) 2025

5) 380   7) 630   6) 5184   3) 2397   4) 280

Improve Your Math Fluency Series

Time: _____   Score: _____

$4\overline{)1524}$ $7\overline{)413}$ $9\overline{)729}$ $6\overline{)3708}$ $2\overline{)84}$

$6\overline{)252}$ $5\overline{)175}$ $3\overline{)609}$ $2\overline{)196}$ $3\overline{)102}$

$4\overline{)880}$ $8\overline{)1552}$ $5\overline{)450}$ $3\overline{)2637}$ $7\overline{)651}$

Part 3: Practice Division with Double-Digit Divisors

Double-digit divisors: In this chapter, the divisor is a two-digit number.

Step-by-step examples:

❶ The 24 doesn't go into 8, so don't write a number above the 8 of 816. ❷ Look at 81 instead of 8. ❸ The largest number 24 can make that doesn't exceed 81 is 72. ❹ Write 72 below 81. ❺ Since 24 times 3 equals 72, write a 3 above the 1 of 816. ❻ Subtract 72 from 81 to make 9. ❼ Bring down the 6 to make 96. ❽ Next, 24 divides evenly into 96. ❾ Write 96 below 96. ❿ Since 24 times 4 equals 96, write a 4 above the 6 of 816. ⓫ Subtract 96 from 96 to make 0.

$$
\begin{array}{r}
3 \\
24\overline{)816} \\
72 \\
\end{array}
\quad
\begin{array}{r}
3 \\
24\overline{)816} \\
72 \\
\hline
96 \\
\end{array}
\quad
\begin{array}{r}
3 \\
24\overline{)816} \\
72 \\
\hline
96 \\
\end{array}
\quad
\begin{array}{r}
34 \\
24\overline{)816} \\
72 \\
\hline
96 \\
96 \\
\hline
0 \\
\end{array}
$$

❶ The 78 doesn't go into 2 or 28, so don't write a number above the 2 or 8 of 28,782. ❷ Look at 287 instead of 2 or 28. ❸ The largest number 78 can make that doesn't exceed 287 is 234. ❹ Write 234 below 287. ❺ Since 78 times 3 equals 234, write a 3 above the 7 of 28,782. ❻ Subtract 234 from 287 to make 53. ❼ Bring down the 8 to make 538. ❽ The largest number 78 can make that doesn't exceed 538 is 468. ❾ Write 468 below 538. ❿ Since 78 times 6 equals 468, write a 6 above the 8 of 28,782. ⓫ Subtract 468 from 538 to make 70. ⓬ Bring down the 2 to make 702. ⓭ Next, 78 divides evenly into 702. ⓮ Write 702 below 702. ⓯ Since 78 times 9 equals 702, write a 9 above the 2 of 28,782. ⓰ Subtract 702 from 702 to make 0.

$$
\begin{array}{r}
3 \\
78\overline{)28782} \\
234 \\
\end{array}
\quad
\begin{array}{r}
3 \\
78\overline{)28782} \\
234 \\
\hline
53 \\
\end{array}
\quad
\begin{array}{r}
36 \\
78\overline{)28782} \\
234 \\
\hline
538 \\
\end{array}
\quad
\begin{array}{r}
36 \\
78\overline{)28782} \\
234 \\
\hline
538 \\
468 \\
\hline
70 \\
\end{array}
\quad
\begin{array}{r}
369 \\
78\overline{)28782} \\
234 \\
\hline
538 \\
468 \\
\hline
702 \\
702 \\
\end{array}
\quad
\begin{array}{r}
369 \\
78\overline{)28782} \\
234 \\
\hline
538 \\
468 \\
\hline
702 \\
702 \\
\hline
0 \\
\end{array}
$$

Guide: Refer to the examples above and use them as a guide. Check your answers to make sure that you are practicing correctly. Once you get the hang of it, try to solve the problems without looking at the examples. Practice this chapter until you become fluent.

Improve Your Math Fluency Series

Time: _____   Score: _____

60) 5280   62) 11284   71) 3337   76) 7372

99) 65043   69) 23598   14) 196   51) 31620

73) 57670   41) 1599   49) 2940   21) 819

Master Long Division with Remainders Practice Workbook

Time: _____ Score: _____

$88\overline{)6952}$ $17\overline{)1292}$ $52\overline{)1404}$ $33\overline{)1815}$

$16\overline{)3728}$ $97\overline{)8633}$ $34\overline{)2414}$ $81\overline{)40176}$

$88\overline{)8624}$ $99\overline{)8316}$ $41\overline{)29766}$ $66\overline{)990}$

Improve Your Math Fluency Series

Time: _____   Score: _____

46) 16560   84) 10248   82) 66420   66) 36828

15) 1260   96) 40992   26) 3224   40) 2080

69) 6348   99) 50886   36) 17568   79) 6636

Master Long Division with Remainders Practice Workbook

Time: _____   Score: _____

86) 946   61) 2562   12) 6456   45) 26775

59) 3245   52) 34424   71) 852   98) 61152

78) 39000   61) 3782   30) 12420   72) 6120

Improve Your Math Fluency Series

Time: _____ Score: _____

60) 52020   15) 1050   47) 31866   50) 19600

61) 16165   15) 225   93) 8277   80) 4640

80) 49440   86) 68370   42) 3024   59) 4248

Master Long Division with Remainders Practice Workbook

Time: _____   Score: _____

42) 2436   35) 31360   96) 9312   71) 68586

26) 338   53) 26659   57) 627   82) 19844

99) 3267   34) 1122   34) 2788   76) 4180

Improve Your Math Fluency Series

Time: _____   Score: _____

57) 27018   54) 7290   40) 3120   79) 2844

99) 81873   13) 2457   56) 5376   44) 40260

83) 76360   33) 21549   49) 833   44) 2552

Master Long Division with Remainders Practice Workbook

Time: _____   Score: _____

61)27206   78)780   55)3355   38)608

31)28830   87)74559   24)1416   91)8645

86)17974   36)16200   80)5360   16)11056

Improve Your Math Fluency Series

Time: _____   Score: _____

27)11556   14)8848   99)77715   95)6745

51)39321   23)14191   29)2610   46)2668

92)8004   59)57702   78)7722   79)13825

Master Long Division with Remainders Practice Workbook

Time: _____   Score: _____

68) 3128   66) 37092   19) 13471   86) 4042

43) 3655   28) 20720   79) 69678   40) 13400

40) 1320   64) 37376   50) 7450   21) 19467

Improve Your Math Fluency Series

Time: _____   Score: _____

$73\overline{)47377}$ $52\overline{)1196}$ $93\overline{)1302}$ $28\overline{)20132}$

$34\overline{)3128}$ $67\overline{)4422}$ $40\overline{)32160}$ $21\overline{)7707}$

$66\overline{)1518}$ $36\overline{)21708}$ $31\overline{)9889}$ $73\overline{)5840}$

Master Long Division with Remainders Practice Workbook

Time: _____   Score: _____

29) 26448   35) 26215   39) 624   77) 1925

84) 3024   62) 15996   33) 16533   53) 2544

21) 20727   85) 4335   59) 15045   21) 18249

Improve Your Math Fluency Series

Time: _____   Score: _____

92) 19596   37) 3182   11) 7524   69) 5865

95) 28690   31) 2542   71) 20448   92) 88596

54) 38286   71) 6035   63) 756   80) 5120

Master Long Division with Remainders Practice Workbook

Time: _____ Score: _____

16) 3360   51) 17493   11) 10395   94) 2350

11) 913   95) 69825   68) 4148   41) 2378

35) 12950   76) 2508   54) 20736   25) 1225

Improve Your Math Fluency Series

Time: _____   Score: _____

14) 1162   82) 2296   58) 31552   63) 47754

89) 20826   96) 7872   21) 16863   60) 1800

50) 2250   96) 6528   97) 7178   30) 1680

Master Long Division with Remainders Practice Workbook

Time: _____   Score: _____

31) 30566   80) 800   83) 5727   62) 49166

66) 858   86) 5074   21) 5670   51) 3570

95) 91295   80) 57680   32) 768   13) 2782

Improve Your Math Fluency Series

Time: _____   Score: _____

86) 1118   12) 5436   52) 15496   90) 83520

87) 6786   98) 3332   57) 3534   71) 852

34) 12954   35) 13825   16) 12832   95) 23560

Master Long Division with Remainders Practice Workbook

Time: _____   Score: _____

$18 \overline{)5742}$ $79 \overline{)2054}$ $91 \overline{)46137}$ $64 \overline{)14976}$

$66 \overline{)45672}$ $86 \overline{)13760}$ $36 \overline{)2376}$ $82 \overline{)5740}$

$74 \overline{)1110}$ $56 \overline{)55944}$ $88 \overline{)38280}$ $76 \overline{)2280}$

Improve Your Math Fluency Series

Time: _____   Score: _____

62) 14012   55) 4345   12) 5172   90) 1800

44) 3740   66) 13002   37) 2146   84) 8064

79) 41870   37) 2997   14) 1232   11) 473

Master Long Division with Remainders Practice Workbook

Time: _____   Score: _____

56) 560   96) 74496   84) 11088   18) 11556

17) 11781   17) 1037   94) 18988   88) 64592

66) 34452   42) 3570   38) 27778   57) 3705

Improve Your Math Fluency Series

Time: _____ Score: _____

52) 3640   47) 3008   72) 1008   26) 2158

38) 874   72) 52416   89) 6853   14) 7294

53) 18020   43) 989   49) 15582   41) 1763

Master Long Division with Remainders Practice Workbook

Time: _____   Score: _____

$90\overline{)8010}$ $14\overline{)1190}$ $69\overline{)64446}$ $22\overline{)1298}$

$99\overline{)56331}$ $15\overline{)2280}$ $29\overline{)1276}$ $73\overline{)876}$

$41\overline{)36080}$ $57\overline{)3249}$ $33\overline{)6798}$ $71\overline{)34719}$

Improve Your Math Fluency Series

Time: _____   Score: _____

$89 \overline{)5162}$ $40 \overline{)6640}$ $22 \overline{)1584}$ $60 \overline{)3120}$

$81 \overline{)4455}$ $42 \overline{)6930}$ $95 \overline{)9310}$ $62 \overline{)55118}$

$33 \overline{)13596}$ $74 \overline{)3552}$ $53 \overline{)5141}$ $68 \overline{)53244}$

Master Long Division with Remainders Practice Workbook

Time: _____   Score: _____

43) 2021   54) 25812   87) 7482   71) 59853

93) 13578   60) 18960   37) 27343   40) 3320

13) 12610   38) 5776   88) 26752   91) 3094

Part 4: Practice Basic Remainder Problems

Division facts with remainders: This chapter introduces the concept of remainders, beginning with the basic division facts.

Remainders: Sometimes, the divisor doesn't evenly divide into the dividend. When this happens, the quotient includes a remainder. The remainder is the part that is left over.

For example, consider 21 divided by 9. If you try 9 times 3, it's too big (27 is greater than 21), and if you try 9 times 2, it's too small (18 is less than 21). Put another way, 9 doesn't evenly divide into 21. If you multiply 9 by 2, there is a remainder of 3. In this example, the quotient is expressed as 2R3. This means that the answer is 2 with a remainder of 3.

Instructions: First, find the largest number that the divisor can make without exceeding the dividend. Then subtract this largest number from the dividend to determine the remainder. Express the quotient with the remainder using remainder notation.

Examples:

$4\overline{)23}$ = 5R3
The largest number that 4 can make that doesn't exceed 23 is 20.
4 times 5 equals 20. The remainder is 23 minus 20, which is 3.
The answer is 5R3.

$6\overline{)20}$ = 3R2
The largest number that 6 can make that doesn't exceed 20 is 18.
6 times 3 equals 18. The remainder is 20 minus 18, which is 2.
The answer is 3R2.

$8\overline{)49}$ = 6R1
The largest number that 8 can make that doesn't exceed 49 is 48.
8 times 6 equals 48. The remainder is 49 minus 48, which is 1.
The answer is 6R1.

Guide: Refer to the examples above and use them as a guide. Check your answers to make sure that you are practicing correctly. Once you get the hang of it, try to solve the problems without looking at the examples. Practice this chapter until you become fluent.

Master Long Division with Remainders Practice Workbook

Time: _____ Score: _____

5)21	9)41	4)38	2)13	7)38	9)84
6)29	6)17	6)14	9)78	6)44	6)55
2)15	2)7	9)66	8)21	3)23	7)27
4)27	9)57	7)48	7)64	3)25	3)22
6)39	8)71	8)55	8)71	2)9	6)22
9)78	6)53	7)51	9)37	2)9	3)19
8)36	2)19	6)43	9)21	2)11	5)23
9)46	9)62	7)32	3)19	4)38	4)15
3)16	7)32	9)59	5)17	4)13	9)22
9)43	6)28	4)39	3)28	3)8	3)22
9)29	2)15	7)26	2)19	7)32	4)25
9)84	3)25	9)21	4)15	9)67	9)51

Improve Your Math Fluency Series

Time: _____   Score: _____

8)20	5)42	4)9	8)55	7)36	7)52
3)29	7)65	3)19	3)8	5)46	7)20
4)15	9)74	7)31	9)67	8)20	8)59
6)20	7)66	6)33	9)43	8)17	8)44
6)35	3)13	9)44	9)19	9)70	5)44
4)22	5)42	4)9	3)29	3)8	6)34
3)20	7)38	2)17	8)45	6)14	2)15
4)18	9)25	9)26	2)11	9)84	6)39
5)39	7)32	5)12	3)17	7)33	3)19
7)57	6)23	3)25	2)17	7)68	7)32
2)19	5)42	8)74	9)64	8)26	2)9
7)18	4)30	9)37	2)15	8)23	2)5

Master Long Division with Remainders Practice Workbook

Time: _____   Score: _____

$9\overline{)37}$ $\quad$ $2\overline{)19}$ $\quad$ $4\overline{)21}$ $\quad$ $8\overline{)43}$ $\quad$ $2\overline{)13}$ $\quad$ $2\overline{)7}$

$7\overline{)37}$ $\quad$ $8\overline{)19}$ $\quad$ $6\overline{)32}$ $\quad$ $3\overline{)25}$ $\quad$ $6\overline{)37}$ $\quad$ $8\overline{)60}$

$5\overline{)31}$ $\quad$ $4\overline{)18}$ $\quad$ $9\overline{)33}$ $\quad$ $7\overline{)57}$ $\quad$ $2\overline{)5}$ $\quad$ $4\overline{)30}$

$8\overline{)46}$ $\quad$ $4\overline{)18}$ $\quad$ $5\overline{)11}$ $\quad$ $5\overline{)47}$ $\quad$ $7\overline{)52}$ $\quad$ $3\overline{)26}$

$7\overline{)68}$ $\quad$ $9\overline{)64}$ $\quad$ $8\overline{)18}$ $\quad$ $5\overline{)14}$ $\quad$ $2\overline{)9}$ $\quad$ $2\overline{)19}$

$3\overline{)20}$ $\quad$ $5\overline{)32}$ $\quad$ $9\overline{)44}$ $\quad$ $9\overline{)60}$ $\quad$ $8\overline{)23}$ $\quad$ $6\overline{)16}$

$3\overline{)13}$ $\quad$ $9\overline{)58}$ $\quad$ $4\overline{)27}$ $\quad$ $3\overline{)17}$ $\quad$ $6\overline{)47}$ $\quad$ $6\overline{)28}$

$6\overline{)29}$ $\quad$ $2\overline{)17}$ $\quad$ $9\overline{)75}$ $\quad$ $8\overline{)68}$ $\quad$ $7\overline{)26}$ $\quad$ $5\overline{)34}$

$3\overline{)13}$ $\quad$ $8\overline{)25}$ $\quad$ $8\overline{)59}$ $\quad$ $7\overline{)18}$ $\quad$ $3\overline{)19}$ $\quad$ $2\overline{)11}$

$7\overline{)69}$ $\quad$ $6\overline{)56}$ $\quad$ $8\overline{)74}$ $\quad$ $6\overline{)47}$ $\quad$ $5\overline{)19}$ $\quad$ $7\overline{)19}$

$7\overline{)33}$ $\quad$ $2\overline{)11}$ $\quad$ $9\overline{)29}$ $\quad$ $3\overline{)26}$ $\quad$ $9\overline{)35}$ $\quad$ $2\overline{)13}$

$3\overline{)25}$ $\quad$ $8\overline{)35}$ $\quad$ $6\overline{)19}$ $\quad$ $3\overline{)26}$ $\quad$ $4\overline{)22}$ $\quad$ $8\overline{)54}$

Improve Your Math Fluency Series

Time: _____   Score: _____

$9\overline{)20}$	$8\overline{)65}$	$2\overline{)7}$	$9\overline{)37}$	$2\overline{)15}$	$9\overline{)87}$
$4\overline{)9}$	$8\overline{)31}$	$8\overline{)52}$	$5\overline{)46}$	$7\overline{)19}$	$9\overline{)68}$
$3\overline{)23}$	$7\overline{)39}$	$3\overline{)25}$	$8\overline{)66}$	$5\overline{)31}$	$3\overline{)14}$
$2\overline{)7}$	$7\overline{)43}$	$5\overline{)29}$	$2\overline{)15}$	$6\overline{)38}$	$3\overline{)19}$
$5\overline{)28}$	$9\overline{)26}$	$5\overline{)17}$	$7\overline{)52}$	$5\overline{)26}$	$8\overline{)18}$
$6\overline{)17}$	$8\overline{)29}$	$6\overline{)28}$	$5\overline{)36}$	$8\overline{)17}$	$9\overline{)20}$
$2\overline{)19}$	$7\overline{)37}$	$9\overline{)88}$	$2\overline{)19}$	$7\overline{)68}$	$7\overline{)34}$
$7\overline{)20}$	$4\overline{)22}$	$9\overline{)26}$	$7\overline{)27}$	$2\overline{)17}$	$7\overline{)41}$
$8\overline{)31}$	$6\overline{)43}$	$9\overline{)40}$	$4\overline{)14}$	$5\overline{)18}$	$6\overline{)17}$
$9\overline{)29}$	$4\overline{)39}$	$8\overline{)39}$	$7\overline{)24}$	$4\overline{)35}$	$8\overline{)73}$
$3\overline{)29}$	$7\overline{)19}$	$4\overline{)25}$	$2\overline{)7}$	$2\overline{)11}$	$4\overline{)19}$
$4\overline{)38}$	$4\overline{)29}$	$4\overline{)37}$	$7\overline{)15}$	$5\overline{)46}$	$9\overline{)55}$

Master Long Division with Remainders Practice Workbook

Time: _____ Score: _____

4)14	7)68	6)29	4)11	9)29	6)56
9)50	5)19	8)58	5)21	9)82	7)55
8)44	5)44	2)19	4)31	2)9	4)9
7)64	6)14	7)66	3)17	7)48	2)11
2)9	7)44	8)44	6)34	2)17	6)49
6)15	2)15	6)55	7)33	7)58	6)56
4)33	7)64	4)19	8)17	5)34	6)50
7)27	7)29	9)69	2)15	6)41	7)48
5)46	2)9	6)55	5)43	7)52	3)17
4)34	8)22	4)14	6)56	9)46	7)43
4)29	6)59	9)76	2)13	9)82	6)16
3)17	3)13	2)15	3)8	5)27	3)16

Improve Your Math Fluency Series

Time: _____   Score: _____

8)44	3)26	3)10	6)57	5)46	8)76
4)39	3)29	3)19	7)67	3)7	8)20
4)33	9)24	8)38	7)41	9)48	4)37
8)27	7)16	5)38	2)19	5)12	3)8
6)39	9)46	4)11	7)16	3)25	5)14
5)47	5)41	6)13	5)21	3)8	8)23
4)31	5)13	8)42	7)54	3)8	6)35
4)30	4)35	6)45	8)33	8)59	4)34
9)42	3)14	7)69	4)33	4)31	4)34
9)62	3)25	2)5	9)28	9)60	6)38
7)41	9)57	7)46	5)47	4)26	7)40
6)17	3)8	5)28	8)22	7)59	9)75

Master Long Division with Remainders Practice Workbook

Time: _____ Score: _____

9)53	4)38	9)42	6)49	6)38	8)65
4)39	6)21	9)74	6)37	4)23	8)69
4)10	3)8	9)60	7)27	8)78	3)14
7)65	4)29	3)17	7)33	7)69	5)24
4)38	9)75	8)21	7)30	8)28	4)33
7)31	6)17	4)15	9)40	8)17	4)30
2)7	7)60	5)39	9)76	2)15	3)22
9)69	8)75	5)12	2)13	4)25	9)40
5)29	4)25	6)28	7)26	3)13	4)27
5)47	2)9	4)30	4)33	6)57	9)30
9)69	6)56	6)20	6)20	4)18	7)66
8)50	9)61	6)55	3)28	7)45	3)14

Improve Your Math Fluency Series

Time: _____   Score: _____

3)10	8)21	8)52	6)29	8)78	2)19
7)18	2)9	4)29	9)21	2)19	2)13
4)37	5)49	4)9	2)15	3)19	6)17
8)61	4)39	4)31	8)18	8)18	8)20
3)7	9)83	9)84	2)13	7)45	5)14
4)23	8)45	8)50	6)40	3)11	8)35
6)34	9)64	4)19	4)22	9)47	7)64
7)39	9)37	6)25	2)19	2)7	3)16
2)17	7)32	2)7	5)44	9)49	7)16
7)30	8)66	3)22	2)5	6)38	9)73
9)19	2)11	7)65	5)21	8)23	6)19
9)58	5)42	6)29	7)33	7)62	5)31

Master Long Division with Remainders Practice Workbook

Time: _____   Score: _____

9)56	8)76	9)34	2)13	5)33	6)13
8)34	4)19	9)41	2)9	3)8	7)26
3)28	5)47	3)25	7)48	2)13	2)9
5)28	5)24	9)48	7)34	4)22	4)22
9)55	4)15	2)19	3)10	5)27	3)26
9)59	8)18	5)31	7)46	6)33	5)34
5)49	7)40	4)17	6)16	5)29	7)41
6)55	4)35	6)56	7)59	6)50	7)27
9)42	4)23	8)53	8)39	2)13	7)57
3)16	4)37	2)19	8)26	5)19	2)13
7)43	6)33	5)39	2)19	3)10	8)74
5)39	4)30	3)13	8)68	9)69	2)9

Improve Your Math Fluency Series

Time: _____   Score: _____

3)20	8)44	4)34	3)25	6)20	6)34
5)42	4)33	2)15	4)13	9)29	2)19
6)38	3)28	9)41	6)32	9)65	2)9
9)71	9)38	5)49	7)31	2)13	6)27
9)80	4)39	5)37	8)39	9)48	2)13
3)20	7)64	7)54	5)46	3)17	6)23
9)35	2)7	9)34	6)35	6)56	7)69
4)13	3)29	9)46	4)13	8)27	5)22
5)42	7)34	2)19	6)14	3)13	4)9
2)7	6)15	4)15	4)9	7)62	7)68
4)13	4)30	3)26	6)13	2)13	9)37
9)22	2)5	8)20	3)28	5)32	7)26

Master Long Division with Remainders Practice Workbook

Time: _____   Score: _____

2)19	4)13	6)39	4)10	8)75	7)43
9)61	4)33	6)38	3)26	6)31	2)11
8)69	9)29	7)66	8)53	9)60	2)13
7)67	5)21	7)46	5)34	3)16	8)58
6)56	2)5	8)19	9)49	5)36	7)30
2)17	9)85	3)29	6)39	9)76	9)89
6)33	2)7	8)36	2)7	2)11	6)27
5)26	6)28	7)44	9)61	6)25	6)39
8)59	5)32	8)46	9)23	3)14	7)58
3)8	5)13	4)31	9)83	2)13	9)20
9)66	5)13	3)25	3)8	4)22	3)28
3)19	7)30	9)42	2)13	9)67	2)9

Improve Your Math Fluency Series

Time: _____   Score: _____

9)32	6)22	9)78	7)36	9)53	8)55
9)80	7)23	8)76	3)28	9)65	9)32
3)17	8)36	5)12	2)13	3)28	4)38
7)36	3)25	6)49	7)23	6)19	4)25
6)27	9)68	8)78	2)11	6)52	4)19
6)13	7)25	2)5	6)19	7)40	3)23
3)25	6)22	4)13	4)31	5)42	4)30
8)77	6)45	9)53	6)45	9)19	6)14
9)64	4)10	7)55	7)44	8)74	6)29
9)84	8)36	3)14	7)37	9)68	6)55
7)58	6)41	6)15	4)11	6)28	5)23
7)58	8)63	3)22	4)30	3)10	2)7

Master Long Division with Remainders Practice Workbook

Time: _____   Score: _____

7)19	5)12	5)43	4)13	8)19	7)45
3)25	6)35	8)22	4)13	3)25	4)15
7)22	6)47	8)66	3)29	4)13	3)26
5)33	8)55	6)13	2)11	4)25	9)68
6)45	7)18	7)32	8)66	8)37	5)12
8)50	7)22	5)46	3)22	9)37	6)51
6)56	3)23	3)19	9)89	7)29	6)43
4)21	5)31	4)18	5)32	7)53	3)29
2)17	3)19	2)13	5)44	3)28	9)43
3)22	2)11	8)49	9)38	2)5	8)25
3)23	8)45	7)46	7)47	9)44	8)75
6)15	9)61	6)49	9)47	8)61	2)5

Improve Your Math Fluency Series

Time: _____   Score: _____

9)48	3)13	2)11	3)17	4)35	6)39
5)43	4)21	8)25	8)69	6)23	9)88
5)44	8)25	7)60	4)9	2)19	5)49
3)26	9)23	8)65	8)33	3)14	7)31
8)25	9)62	2)9	5)41	6)58	6)46
5)17	4)23	6)33	3)19	8)46	8)42
2)5	7)20	9)39	9)32	5)14	2)15
6)14	4)37	4)15	7)52	4)11	3)29
8)17	8)58	4)22	8)27	9)37	7)43
9)53	2)13	4)35	4)25	9)67	4)30
2)7	3)16	6)50	5)29	4)17	6)27
7)66	7)48	3)25	6)25	8)34	2)11

Master Long Division with Remainders Practice Workbook

Time: _____   Score: _____

6)14	4)14	9)68	5)21	3)11	6)34
8)36	6)33	5)28	4)38	9)39	4)31
5)22	4)23	3)14	7)55	4)27	2)17
5)34	3)13	4)39	8)59	3)13	7)15
7)69	3)22	5)18	9)25	6)43	9)70
8)60	9)33	6)55	5)21	5)22	8)52
9)64	8)45	2)13	3)22	9)34	6)34
9)61	3)10	5)19	3)19	5)18	5)46
7)45	7)64	7)33	3)10	9)85	4)9
7)20	2)19	6)16	7)27	2)13	6)19
9)59	9)25	4)26	4)19	8)78	5)16
9)71	6)53	3)16	8)55	9)24	9)22

Improve Your Math Fluency Series

Time: _____   Score: _____

3)13	3)28	9)83	9)73	7)38	7)22
4)30	3)19	2)15	8)71	8)23	8)74
7)52	3)23	7)59	8)55	2)19	8)49
7)23	2)7	2)5	6)31	6)13	7)46
2)13	4)31	2)9	7)57	7)68	5)18
9)56	3)11	5)23	4)22	5)21	7)43
7)30	3)14	4)14	2)13	2)17	4)10
8)47	5)47	2)19	5)27	7)41	7)45
2)15	3)22	3)7	4)37	5)47	3)29
4)27	9)56	9)19	7)38	4)23	6)16
6)56	8)44	8)76	4)15	5)19	5)21
8)31	6)51	8)46	8)49	8)71	8)20

Master Long Division with Remainders Practice Workbook

Time: _____   Score: _____

4)22	3)8	6)37	9)62	2)19	5)49
3)13	7)45	2)7	3)22	9)71	5)49
4)11	2)11	2)5	6)26	4)35	8)52
8)17	2)19	7)19	5)14	2)17	6)44
9)22	3)7	8)52	4)18	5)13	8)74
6)57	3)29	6)34	7)55	2)11	2)13
3)17	6)38	6)13	2)9	7)62	7)43
5)11	8)52	4)14	5)48	6)43	7)54
2)5	5)13	9)68	7)25	3)23	4)33
2)15	5)14	5)49	8)77	7)59	9)84
6)21	6)50	3)26	4)15	6)55	9)25
2)9	6)33	7)66	3)13	9)87	2)5

Improve Your Math Fluency Series

Time: _____   Score: _____

5)39	7)59	7)69	7)37	3)20	7)50
5)42	3)16	9)51	4)11	2)7	8)52
9)34	6)38	6)20	3)22	2)17	7)37
3)16	3)20	3)13	3)7	2)7	6)14
6)28	4)18	8)76	9)70	3)29	5)48
9)67	9)75	7)48	3)23	7)60	5)24
9)20	9)26	3)25	7)47	3)19	3)22
3)14	9)44	4)15	2)17	2)15	7)52
4)26	4)35	4)31	8)29	7)57	6)50
5)32	7)61	8)63	7)51	4)10	4)29
9)50	3)28	5)37	6)33	9)62	7)36
9)73	7)66	6)45	4)11	7)59	3)13

Master Long Division with Remainders Practice Workbook

Time: _____   Score: _____

6)53	9)77	2)13	3)10	2)7	2)13
9)88	5)24	5)41	7)61	9)33	6)35
9)24	7)40	7)57	7)52	5)18	5)29
8)35	9)56	6)14	3)11	8)35	2)7
5)11	9)20	2)11	2)13	2)15	5)13
4)18	5)21	9)58	9)61	6)57	2)11
2)17	5)39	4)18	5)29	8)53	3)19
8)41	8)69	4)30	6)32	2)9	8)73
5)49	5)22	7)67	4)11	6)22	5)41
8)51	6)16	2)13	7)50	2)19	8)55
8)34	8)75	7)17	5)24	4)17	5)18
3)28	3)14	9)35	2)17	9)30	8)42

Improve Your Math Fluency Series

Time: _____   Score: _____

2)19	6)47	9)77	8)54	8)77	5)31
2)11	4)35	9)79	4)39	5)24	3)17
9)74	6)52	8)36	7)19	8)20	6)38
8)70	4)30	6)40	3)19	7)37	2)15
3)22	6)25	9)89	9)88	4)9	5)42
8)20	6)21	7)59	7)67	3)20	9)42
5)17	6)38	6)23	3)26	4)30	6)34
7)31	9)30	7)26	2)7	3)29	4)22
7)20	3)22	7)29	2)15	6)46	4)35
8)63	9)75	5)43	4)22	8)35	7)37
4)37	5)22	9)88	8)78	3)23	7)18
3)8	8)71	5)17	3)16	4)10	6)58

Master Long Division with Remainders Practice Workbook

Time: _____ Score: _____

$9\overline{)40}$ $3\overline{)22}$ $5\overline{)17}$ $4\overline{)38}$ $8\overline{)23}$ $6\overline{)34}$

$8\overline{)57}$ $7\overline{)69}$ $4\overline{)39}$ $5\overline{)33}$ $3\overline{)7}$ $2\overline{)11}$

$5\overline{)28}$ $6\overline{)23}$ $3\overline{)23}$ $3\overline{)19}$ $2\overline{)13}$ $4\overline{)23}$

$5\overline{)17}$ $9\overline{)52}$ $7\overline{)27}$ $4\overline{)37}$ $3\overline{)26}$ $4\overline{)30}$

$6\overline{)32}$ $2\overline{)9}$ $9\overline{)58}$ $7\overline{)25}$ $8\overline{)51}$ $5\overline{)49}$

$6\overline{)32}$ $3\overline{)26}$ $2\overline{)17}$ $9\overline{)22}$ $4\overline{)9}$ $4\overline{)17}$

$6\overline{)50}$ $3\overline{)13}$ $2\overline{)9}$ $9\overline{)82}$ $3\overline{)26}$ $4\overline{)13}$

$6\overline{)22}$ $7\overline{)47}$ $5\overline{)32}$ $3\overline{)17}$ $8\overline{)35}$ $8\overline{)62}$

$9\overline{)88}$ $8\overline{)55}$ $4\overline{)13}$ $9\overline{)48}$ $4\overline{)38}$ $5\overline{)36}$

$8\overline{)44}$ $6\overline{)50}$ $4\overline{)17}$ $6\overline{)53}$ $5\overline{)17}$ $7\overline{)43}$

$7\overline{)40}$ $6\overline{)53}$ $3\overline{)23}$ $6\overline{)21}$ $2\overline{)5}$ $2\overline{)7}$

$4\overline{)26}$ $6\overline{)58}$ $8\overline{)74}$ $3\overline{)28}$ $7\overline{)43}$ $9\overline{)42}$

Improve Your Math Fluency Series

Time: _____   Score: _____

4)34	3)19	3)17	7)20	5)36	6)35
3)23	5)11	2)19	4)22	3)14	4)35
4)18	4)29	6)55	4)38	6)31	9)38
8)61	4)31	6)23	9)44	7)52	7)65
8)41	2)9	8)61	3)16	9)49	8)65
6)35	8)68	7)65	2)17	6)33	8)21
6)43	3)20	4)38	8)44	8)61	2)19
4)29	2)7	2)7	6)53	4)10	4)19
6)58	2)13	7)51	7)39	9)70	3)8
8)62	7)22	8)19	5)14	3)26	3)13
3)26	5)27	7)65	4)18	7)62	9)67
3)16	7)45	2)7	7)20	7)47	6)33

Master Long Division with Remainders Practice Workbook

Time: _____   Score: _____

6)59	8)70	6)44	4)14	3)29	8)26
6)45	4)38	5)21	7)53	7)59	6)23
9)46	4)22	3)11	8)59	3)23	9)26
9)33	4)33	3)13	4)22	6)44	9)34
5)12	2)15	6)34	9)70	4)15	3)29
3)22	8)18	5)14	3)14	4)14	6)41
8)19	3)26	2)9	9)71	2)5	8)20
4)15	4)9	5)47	5)32	3)14	5)39
4)31	7)48	8)39	6)59	6)38	4)37
5)13	4)35	7)38	9)59	5)23	2)17
9)75	2)13	5)29	8)35	4)39	2)7
4)29	5)16	9)56	5)27	9)55	3)23

Improve Your Math Fluency Series

Time: _____   Score: _____

3)10	2)11	4)11	6)37	8)29	5)11
3)14	5)28	4)29	2)19	4)27	9)22
7)32	6)39	9)32	8)39	4)27	4)13
2)13	9)25	4)37	9)35	5)42	4)19
8)35	4)38	6)37	7)50	3)19	3)7
5)33	9)39	8)46	4)17	4)29	8)18
7)19	8)50	3)8	7)23	8)39	8)44
8)26	3)25	7)58	9)82	2)7	8)34
8)75	9)29	4)33	6)58	5)12	5)12
6)46	2)19	9)53	2)5	7)50	3)20
9)35	2)5	7)15	6)59	8)55	5)16
6)32	3)20	7)31	6)16	5)21	4)34

Part 5: Practice Remainders with Single-Digit Divisors

Step-by-step examples:

❶ The 6 doesn't go into 4, so don't write a number above the 4 of 459. ❷ Look at 45 instead of 4. ❸ The largest number 6 can make that doesn't exceed 45 is 42. ❹ Write 42 below 45. ❺ Since 6 times 7 equals 42, write a 7 above the 5 of 459. ❻ Subtract 42 from 45 to make 3. ❼ Bring down the 9 to make 39. ❽ The largest number 6 can make that doesn't exceed 39 is 36. ❾ Write 36 below 39. ❿ Since 6 times 6 equals 36, write a 6 above the 9 of 459. ⓫ Subtract 36 from 39 to make 3. ⓬ Write the remainder, 3, after 46.

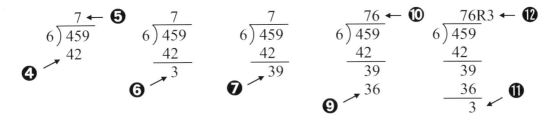

❶ The largest number 2 can make that doesn't exceed 7 is 6. ❷ Write 6 below 7. ❸ Since 2 times 3 equals 6, write a 3 above the 7 of 7513. ❹ Subtract 6 from 7 to make 1. ❺ Bring down the 5 to make 15. ❻ The largest number 2 can make that doesn't exceed 15 is 14. ❼ Write 14 below 15. ❽ Since 2 times 7 equals 14, write a 7 above the 5 of 7513. ❾ Subtract 14 from 15 to make 1. ❿ Bring down the 1 to make 11. ⓫ The largest number 2 can make that doesn't exceed 11 is 10. ⓬ Write 10 below 11. ⓭ Since 2 times 5 equals 10, write a 5 above the 1 of 7513. ⓮ Subtract 10 from 11 to make 1. ⓯ Bring down the 3 to make 13. ⓰ The largest number 2 can make that doesn't exceed 13 is 12. ⓱ Write 12 below 13. ⓲ Since 2 times 6 equals 12, write a 6 above the 3 of 7513. ⓳ Subtract 12 from 13 to make 1. ⓴ Write the remainder, 1, after 3756.

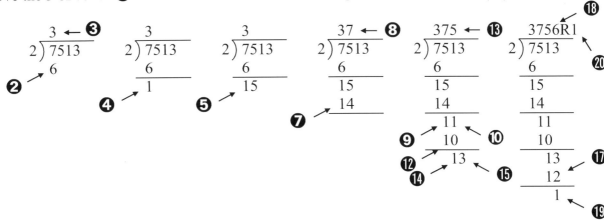

Improve Your Math Fluency Series

Time: _____ Score: _____

$5\overline{)162}$ $5\overline{)474}$ $7\overline{)5246}$ $8\overline{)483}$ $4\overline{)383}$

$4\overline{)3311}$ $5\overline{)487}$ $4\overline{)583}$ $3\overline{)1799}$ $7\overline{)136}$

$8\overline{)641}$ $8\overline{)2274}$ $8\overline{)505}$ $9\overline{)300}$ $6\overline{)83}$

Master Long Division with Remainders Practice Workbook

Time: _____ Score: _____

2) 367   6) 1226   9) 784   6) 5522   6) 5289

5) 54   9) 151   8) 6436 7) 624   6) 3697

3) 40   7) 463   7) 6648 2) 1807   6) 3032

Improve Your Math Fluency Series

Time: _____   Score: _____

$4\overline{)3547}$ $9\overline{)2625}$ $6\overline{)974}$ $8\overline{)3284}$ $6\overline{)5716}$

$3\overline{)53}$ $4\overline{)273}$ $2\overline{)179}$ $4\overline{)3870}$ $6\overline{)2209}$

$8\overline{)2582}$ $7\overline{)292}$ $2\overline{)1273}$ $7\overline{)2431}$ $9\overline{)650}$

Master Long Division with Remainders Practice Workbook

Time: _____ Score: _____

7) 620   7) 4029   8) 6822   7) 4502   7) 2253

6) 4610   8) 742   7) 577   9) 1544   5) 438

3) 2053   8) 6162   5) 329   2) 199   7) 131

Improve Your Math Fluency Series

Time: _____   Score: _____

$2\overline{)71}$ $6\overline{)880}$ $3\overline{)178}$ $7\overline{)6497}$ $4\overline{)3834}$

$2\overline{)435}$ $7\overline{)590}$ $2\overline{)189}$ $4\overline{)3989}$ $7\overline{)253}$

$3\overline{)1342}$ $9\overline{)510}$ $7\overline{)458}$ $5\overline{)184}$ $7\overline{)3943}$

Master Long Division with Remainders Practice Workbook

Time: _____ Score: _____

8) 7033   4) 3815   3) 227   9) 559   9) 3566

4) 285   2) 1071   2) 1047   2) 1393   6) 431

4) 1186   3) 428   5) 348   5) 106   8) 770

Improve Your Math Fluency Series

Time: _____   Score: _____

5) 1061   5) 3856   8) 3479   5) 2804   2) 1183

4) 3819   6) 107   8) 163   4) 305   9) 4601

4) 3490   8) 4747   9) 8075   7) 236   3) 133

Master Long Division with Remainders Practice Workbook

Time: _____   Score: _____

8) 3729   5) 237   5) 3967   7) 578   8) 356

3) 2719   4) 331   8) 6046   4) 81   5) 486

2) 183   6) 4949   4) 89   8) 3524   5) 2462

Improve Your Math Fluency Series

Time: _____   Score: _____

5) 276   7) 534   5) 133   6) 2117   6) 2002

7) 277   6) 212   3) 107   2) 131   2) 39

4) 3155   2) 759   5) 342   4) 3590   6) 392

Master Long Division with Remainders Practice Workbook

Time: _____ Score: _____

4) 298   6) 274   7) 193   5) 332   6) 482

7) 6729   3) 206   9) 860   9) 4924   7) 293

3) 1357   3) 2462   9) 4328   8) 7554   5) 188

Improve Your Math Fluency Series

Time: _____   Score: _____

7)674   6)291   2)69   5)111   6)63

8)7402   5)169   7)3039   8)1868   8)311

6)5167   5)83   2)61   4)187   4)93

Master Long Division with Remainders Practice Workbook

Time: _____ Score: _____

2) 99   8) 371   5) 2863   4) 1423   5) 454

7) 884   4) 3593   5) 107   6) 281   9) 640

7) 4925   8) 571   9) 498   7) 6512   7) 6198

Improve Your Math Fluency Series

Time: _____   Score: _____

$3\overline{)1709}$ $2\overline{)603}$ $5\overline{)1639}$ $6\overline{)5501}$ $6\overline{)179}$

$9\overline{)4933}$ $4\overline{)1559}$ $2\overline{)1849}$ $3\overline{)113}$ $9\overline{)5897}$

$4\overline{)641}$ $2\overline{)899}$ $4\overline{)1346}$ $2\overline{)99}$ $5\overline{)309}$

Master Long Division with Remainders Practice Workbook

Time: _____   Score: _____

$2 \overline{)1691}$ $3 \overline{)293}$ $5 \overline{)4847}$ $6 \overline{)3970}$ $9 \overline{)641}$

$4 \overline{)99}$ $2 \overline{)175}$ $4 \overline{)250}$ $4 \overline{)102}$ $6 \overline{)2018}$

$4 \overline{)70}$ $2 \overline{)1691}$ $6 \overline{)583}$ $4 \overline{)2250}$ $7 \overline{)4468}$

Improve Your Math Fluency Series

Time: _____   Score: _____

$2\overline{)187}$ $2\overline{)169}$ $5\overline{)194}$ $3\overline{)103}$ $4\overline{)306}$

$9\overline{)7894}$ $9\overline{)4157}$ $2\overline{)77}$ $5\overline{)59}$ $5\overline{)66}$

$8\overline{)5366}$ $7\overline{)3469}$ $4\overline{)283}$ $8\overline{)4211}$ $8\overline{)3917}$

Master Long Division with Remainders Practice Workbook

Time: _____   Score: _____

8) 285   4) 3806   4) 905   4) 3590   9) 3223

2) 177   3) 127   5) 1688   6) 575   5) 269

6) 2974   8) 6307   3) 236   7) 2558   2) 595

Improve Your Math Fluency Series

Time: _____   Score: _____

9)6224   8)86   5)4461   6)291   2)503

8)3139   2)105   2)139   7)3336   3)79

6)3058   5)4642   6)381   3)1496   6)1561

Master Long Division with Remainders Practice Workbook

Time: _____   Score: _____

2) 195   4) 3311   6) 5391   6) 5267   9) 524

4) 398   5) 68   7) 302   8) 333   6) 95

6) 437   9) 1994   6) 207   4) 203   2) 75

Improve Your Math Fluency Series

Time: _____ Score: _____

$9\overline{)259}$ $5\overline{)2003}$ $2\overline{)1379}$ $5\overline{)254}$ $6\overline{)5431}$

$5\overline{)2531}$ $9\overline{)197}$ $6\overline{)4221}$ $7\overline{)193}$ $3\overline{)124}$

$7\overline{)4098}$ $3\overline{)539}$ $3\overline{)239}$ $3\overline{)1882}$ $2\overline{)57}$

Master Long Division with Remainders Practice Workbook

Time: _____   Score: _____

7) 4651   6) 2143   4) 258   4) 2366   7) 143

9) 851   8) 6985   5) 2799   2) 827   7) 75

9) 543   7) 1126   2) 111   2) 93   9) 98

Improve Your Math Fluency Series

Time: _____   Score: _____

7) 163   8) 3723   5) 417   2) 1681   3) 214

5) 74   2) 389   2) 1821   3) 2741   9) 656

5) 947   7) 3537   9) 1166   5) 376   4) 293

Master Long Division with Remainders Practice Workbook

Time: _____   Score: _____

$6 \overline{)3845}$ $2 \overline{)297}$ $5 \overline{)2733}$ $8 \overline{)802}$ $9 \overline{)394}$

$3 \overline{)2324}$ $5 \overline{)2013}$ $9 \overline{)7257}$ $6 \overline{)445}$ $6 \overline{)4426}$

$8 \overline{)1330}$ $2 \overline{)23}$ $5 \overline{)4943}$ $7 \overline{)4566}$ $9 \overline{)538}$

Improve Your Math Fluency Series

Time: _____ Score: _____

$9 \overline{)8234}$ $8 \overline{)3062}$ $2 \overline{)1607}$ $3 \overline{)2663}$ $5 \overline{)4732}$

$2 \overline{)161}$ $3 \overline{)41}$ $4 \overline{)74}$ $8 \overline{)186}$ $9 \overline{)886}$

$8 \overline{)131}$ $6 \overline{)194}$ $2 \overline{)37}$ $5 \overline{)156}$ $5 \overline{)438}$

Master Long Division with Remainders Practice Workbook

Time: _____   Score: _____

4) 2017   7) 645   6) 293   6) 1137   4) 323

4) 273   6) 3993   4) 345   5) 493   2) 129

3) 1546   2) 45   2) 1851   9) 6590   8) 6094

Part 6: Practice Multi-Digit Division with Remainders

Step-by-step examples:

❶ The 32 doesn't go into 9, so don't write a number above the 9 of 914. ❷ Look at 91 instead of 9. ❸ The largest number 32 can make that doesn't exceed 91 is 64. ❹ Write 64 below 91. ❺ Since 32 times 2 equals 64, write a 2 above the 1 of 914. ❻ Subtract 64 from 91 to make 27. ❼ Bring down the 4 to make 274. ❽ The largest number 32 can make that doesn't exceed 274 is 256. ❾ Write 256 below 274. ❿ Since 32 times 8 equals 256, write an 8 above the 4 of 914. ⓫ Subtract 256 from 274 to make 18. ⓬ Write the remainder, 18, after 28.

```
      2 ← ❺            2                  2 ← ❿            28R18 ← ⓬
  32)914            32)914             32)914            32)914
❹→ 64                  64                 64                64
                   ❻↗  27            ❼↗ 274               274
                                         256 ← ❾           256
                                                            18 ↙ ⓫
```

❶ The 42 doesn't go into 1 or 10, so don't write a number above the 1 or 0 of 10,356. ❷ Look at 103 instead of 1 or 10. ❸ The largest number 42 can make that doesn't exceed 103 is 84. ❹ Write 84 below 103. ❺ Since 42 times 2 equals 84, write a 2 above the 3 of 10,356. ❻ Subtract 84 from 103 to make 19. ❼ Bring down the 5 to make 195. ❽ The largest number 42 can make that doesn't exceed 195 is 168. ❾ Write 168 below 195. ❿ Since 42 times 4 equals 168, write a 4 above the 5 of 10,356. ⓫ Subtract 168 from 195 to make 27. ⓬ Bring down the 6 to make 276. ⓭ The largest number 42 can make that doesn't exceed 276 is 252. ⓮ Write 252 below 276. ⓯ Since 42 times 6 equals 252, write a 6 above the 6 of 10,356. ⓰ Subtract 252 from 276 to make 24. ⓱ Write the remainder, 24, after 246.

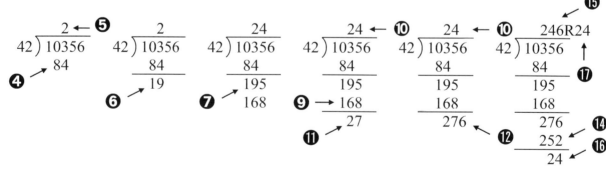

Master Long Division with Remainders Practice Workbook

Time: _____   Score: _____

$64 \overline{)4807}$ $74 \overline{)2445}$ $97 \overline{)8835}$ $34 \overline{)2184}$

$64 \overline{)46787}$ $87 \overline{)6708}$ $21 \overline{)3703}$ $63 \overline{)8131}$

$76 \overline{)17785}$ $59 \overline{)35644}$ $53 \overline{)799}$ $71 \overline{)51621}$

Improve Your Math Fluency Series

Time: _____   Score: _____

$31 \overline{)2024}$ $69 \overline{)39752}$ $37 \overline{)7031}$ $45 \overline{)1713}$

$95 \overline{)6369}$ $92 \overline{)63390}$ $61 \overline{)612}$ $75 \overline{)1732}$

$52 \overline{)13522}$ $29 \overline{)1715}$ $38 \overline{)997}$ $49 \overline{)22154}$

Master Long Division with Remainders Practice Workbook

Time: _____   Score: _____

76) 74789   39) 3129   26) 473   37) 10771

51) 11938   86) 5851   74) 19170   71) 64119

74) 971   91) 49422   93) 24000   20) 6567

Time: _____   Score: _____

$49\overline{)37883}$ $85\overline{)1109}$ $22\overline{)14438}$ $93\overline{)35715}$

$57\overline{)42300}$ $60\overline{)51904}$ $52\overline{)51534}$ $96\overline{)5955}$

$77\overline{)75315}$ $71\overline{)65966}$ $83\overline{)6394}$ $85\overline{)2555}$

Master Long Division with Remainders Practice Workbook

Time: _____ Score: _____

41) 742		87) 40456		91) 43956		68) 818

80) 3848		58) 38050		11) 8604		65) 19701

33) 20890		72) 4615		69) 5391		67) 4626

Improve Your Math Fluency Series

Time: _____ Score: _____

27)4029   31)2731   71)6393   65)50051

22)311   71)47579   95)72019   67)5634

19)15455   95)4566   87)4794   43)10838

Master Long Division with Remainders Practice Workbook

Time: _____ Score: _____

$53 \overline{)34186}$ $10 \overline{)736}$ $91 \overline{)6100}$ $50 \overline{)1953}$

$31 \overline{)14142}$ $57 \overline{)3310}$ $68 \overline{)1368}$ $36 \overline{)35215}$

$10 \overline{)2286}$ $21 \overline{)16742}$ $19 \overline{)8139}$ $97 \overline{)79544}$

Improve Your Math Fluency Series

Time: _____   Score: _____

$55 \overline{)35256}$ $42 \overline{)1142}$ $97 \overline{)4561}$ $43 \overline{)9811}$

$23 \overline{)237}$ $62 \overline{)32990}$ $51 \overline{)18470}$ $70 \overline{)22193}$

$26 \overline{)19036}$ $75 \overline{)32852}$ $72 \overline{)6053}$ $46 \overline{)34462}$

Master Long Division with Remainders Practice Workbook

Time: _____   Score: _____

$54 \overline{)869}$ $54 \overline{)12913}$ $11 \overline{)383}$ $72 \overline{)4831}$

$75 \overline{)22509}$ $27 \overline{)15668}$ $42 \overline{)15001}$ $79 \overline{)7114}$

$89 \overline{)1432}$ $32 \overline{)2370}$ $92 \overline{)8655}$ $14 \overline{)10157}$

Improve Your Math Fluency Series

Time: _____   Score: _____

$95 \overline{)34676}$ $98 \overline{)8821}$ $44 \overline{)40571}$ $34 \overline{)6775}$

$96 \overline{)10566}$ $51 \overline{)38105}$ $50 \overline{)709}$ $51 \overline{)13012}$

$11 \overline{)477}$ $77 \overline{)7323}$ $96 \overline{)965}$ $20 \overline{)587}$

Master Long Division with Remainders Practice Workbook

Time: _____   Score: _____

81) 3485   27) 652   23) 4216   62) 5148

57) 18697   51) 44580   94) 34501   45) 20478

14) 13106   71) 37849   90) 6123   96) 51457

$28 \overline{)24278}$ $\quad$ $48 \overline{)3219}$ $\quad$ $69 \overline{)2970}$ $\quad$ $22 \overline{)14478}$

$97 \overline{)46173}$ $\quad$ $76 \overline{)44089}$ $\quad$ $81 \overline{)50789}$ $\quad$ $81 \overline{)42696}$

$11 \overline{)508}$ $\quad$ $19 \overline{)1260}$ $\quad$ $57 \overline{)2510}$ $\quad$ $54 \overline{)1837}$

Master Long Division with Remainders Practice Workbook

Time: _____   Score: _____

92) 3413   72) 46877   48) 26738   28) 25622

28) 2074   60) 32463   25) 882   21) 2060

68) 46991   10) 481   92) 52263   31) 2794

Improve Your Math Fluency Series

Time: _____   Score: _____

$45 \overline{\smash{)}2884}$ $25 \overline{\smash{)}16903}$ $44 \overline{\smash{)}573}$ $90 \overline{\smash{)}6667}$

$65 \overline{\smash{)}1172}$ $45 \overline{\smash{)}3066}$ $51 \overline{\smash{)}2502}$ $87 \overline{\smash{)}4789}$

$22 \overline{\smash{)}13514}$ $61 \overline{\smash{)}13058}$ $80 \overline{\smash{)}7122}$ $95 \overline{\smash{)}4753}$

Master Long Division with Remainders Practice Workbook

Time: _____   Score: _____

$77 \overline{)11556}$ $94 \overline{)3481}$ $72 \overline{)25425}$ $29 \overline{)11405}$

$87 \overline{)66737}$ $20 \overline{)1689}$ $87 \overline{)31495}$ $69 \overline{)48994}$

$24 \overline{)21891}$ $46 \overline{)2209}$ $51 \overline{)870}$ $66 \overline{)7136}$

Improve Your Math Fluency Series

Time: _____   Score: _____

79) 1032   47) 2641   66) 48909   88) 7047

14) 1165   50) 12651   36) 3461   78) 9834

72) 50545   74) 59357   68) 64470   28) 12385

Master Long Division with Remainders Practice Workbook

Time: _____ Score: _____

34)11767   36)3249   30)21488   74)5331

26)835   34)30876   26)443   53)2072

18)1747   76)4485   57)4682   70)777

Improve Your Math Fluency Series

Time: _____   Score: _____

$73 \overline{)32932}$ $29 \overline{)13552}$ $35 \overline{)2774}$ $77 \overline{)4242}$

$81 \overline{)18639}$ $39 \overline{)26212}$ $19 \overline{)1808}$ $25 \overline{)16006}$

$27 \overline{)276}$ $75 \overline{)33006}$ $41 \overline{)40636}$ $88 \overline{)8014}$

Master Long Division with Remainders Practice Workbook

Time: _____   Score: _____

89) 2766   14) 449   35) 1370   76) 14670

93) 1961   40) 36364   86) 6968   26) 1459

84) 30241   65) 13074   51) 3163   25) 1728

Improve Your Math Fluency Series

Time: _____   Score: _____

$17 \overline{)15800}$ $85 \overline{)6893}$ $54 \overline{)1628}$ $50 \overline{)25057}$

$43 \overline{)30062}$ $44 \overline{)3038}$ $38 \overline{)34851}$ $55 \overline{)3800}$

$10 \overline{)722}$ $98 \overline{)97217}$ $17 \overline{)7789}$ $79 \overline{)5301}$

Master Long Division with Remainders Practice Workbook

Time: _____ Score: _____

68) 43116   43) 4263   87) 6619   65) 5074

32) 28873   97) 20379   82) 67164   39) 10693

57) 3823   84) 10249   26) 5048   51) 25864

Improve Your Math Fluency Series

Time: _____   Score: _____

49) 3972   47) 523   94) 54992   55) 2919

18) 1575   40) 3646   66) 3899   48) 32981

23) 623   52) 2293   57) 4168   38) 35954

Master Long Division with Remainders Practice Workbook

Time: _____   Score: _____

$83 \overline{)36523}$ $57 \overline{)46114}$ $43 \overline{)3272}$ $29 \overline{)25266}$

$12 \overline{)7489}$ $34 \overline{)16088}$ $91 \overline{)8101}$ $87 \overline{)66122}$

$55 \overline{)4073}$ $36 \overline{)2526}$ $54 \overline{)2488}$ $33 \overline{)2775}$

Improve Your Math Fluency Series

Time: _____   Score: _____

$44 \overline{)32568}$ $82 \overline{)44205}$ $97 \overline{)77124}$ $18 \overline{)887}$

$34 \overline{)28630}$ $63 \overline{)11916}$ $57 \overline{)3824}$ $34 \overline{)954}$

$45 \overline{)37038}$ $75 \overline{)6752}$ $65 \overline{)723}$ $65 \overline{)56359}$

Master Long Division with Remainders Practice Workbook

Answer Key

Part 1 Answers

Page 8	Page 11	Page 14	Page 17
6, 7, 2, 8, 6, 4	3, 4, 1, 7, 4, 9	5, 8, 9, 3, 6, 5	6, 2, 7, 2, 3, 4
2, 7, 3, 7, 3, 2	5, 6, 4, 4, 8, 5	3, 1, 9, 2, 9, 7	5, 1, 2, 6, 8, 1
2, 1, 6, 6, 9, 7	5, 9, 4, 5, 3, 1	5, 8, 9, 7, 8, 6	5, 7, 7, 2, 8, 5
4, 3, 1, 7, 9, 6	8, 9, 7, 4, 5, 4	6, 1, 2, 9, 4, 7	7, 9, 6, 9, 2, 6
8, 1, 1, 4, 1, 4	8, 2, 3, 9, 3, 6	1, 1, 2, 9, 5, 3	8, 2, 7, 4, 5, 9
7, 5, 9, 1, 4, 5	5, 3, 2, 3, 2, 4	3, 6, 6, 2, 9, 5	1, 2, 7, 5, 9, 4
2, 5, 2, 1, 3, 4	2, 5, 8, 5, 8, 6	3, 5, 3, 1, 2, 5	7, 2, 6, 2, 2, 7
3, 9, 3, 4, 2, 1	2, 9, 1, 6, 7, 2	5, 1, 6, 5, 5, 1	7, 4, 7, 5, 5, 5
1, 2, 5, 5, 5, 8	1, 1, 2, 4, 3, 8	1, 6, 4, 6, 1, 2	1, 1, 3, 7, 9, 7
3, 7, 4, 8, 8, 6	6, 8, 4, 3, 2, 3	4, 6, 4, 7, 9, 2	4, 4, 4, 8, 6, 3
8, 5, 6, 2, 3, 2	6, 2, 1, 6, 9, 1	5, 1, 4, 2, 1, 8	8, 6, 7, 5, 3, 3
8, 3, 1, 8, 5, 8	8, 6, 1, 1, 2, 1	5, 9, 2, 5, 2, 6	7, 2, 1, 9, 4, 1

Page 9	Page 12	Page 15	Page 18
3, 6, 9, 8, 1, 8	7, 6, 2, 6, 7, 2	8, 3, 5, 4, 7, 3	6, 1, 9, 4, 6, 6
5, 7, 1, 7, 3, 8	5, 4, 3, 9, 4, 9	5, 1, 7, 5, 2, 7	8, 9, 8, 6, 7, 4
2, 2, 1, 4, 8, 3	2, 9, 4, 5, 1, 2	7, 5, 1, 1, 3, 4	9, 2, 3, 9, 3, 7
4, 4, 7, 1, 7, 4	4, 6, 8, 3, 9, 1	3, 2, 6, 9, 9, 8	8, 5, 5, 9, 7, 5
2, 4, 4, 1, 7, 5	4, 4, 7, 7, 3, 2	5, 9, 2, 4, 3, 4	5, 4, 9, 3, 9, 1
9, 2, 9, 5, 2, 3	2, 3, 5, 7, 8, 6	5, 8, 9, 1, 6, 6	1, 5, 6, 2, 3, 2
5, 9, 4, 6, 7, 3	8, 6, 2, 9, 4, 7	9, 8, 2, 4, 6, 8	1, 8, 7, 5, 4, 6
5, 3, 4, 9, 7, 8	6, 8, 9, 7, 6, 2	4, 2, 3, 1, 4, 8	2, 8, 5, 7, 4, 9
3, 4, 2, 9, 5, 4	1, 1, 1, 1, 5, 3	6, 6, 1, 7, 1, 4	3, 3, 2, 2, 1, 6
2, 5, 2, 2, 2, 4	3, 5, 3, 3, 4, 7	2, 2, 4, 1, 5, 9	9, 3, 3, 3, 5, 7
7, 1, 9, 2, 4, 8	7, 7, 9, 2, 3, 1	7, 6, 6, 8, 3, 9	3, 4, 5, 9, 2, 4
8, 2, 5, 1, 9, 2	6, 1, 4, 6, 6, 9	5, 4, 3, 3, 5, 4	3, 1, 8, 6, 3, 6

Page 10	Page 13	Page 16	Page 19
5, 6, 9, 2, 1, 4	1, 9, 7, 1, 5, 2	3, 2, 8, 7, 7, 1	7, 3, 2, 1, 5, 4
1, 9, 8, 4, 8, 9	5, 9, 3, 1, 9, 9	4, 8, 6, 2, 1, 4	5, 8, 2, 7, 7, 7
5, 4, 2, 5, 2, 5	3, 7, 7, 7, 9, 6	9, 3, 2, 7, 3, 8	3, 9, 2, 7, 8, 5
5, 4, 5, 4, 6, 3	7, 6, 3, 1, 4, 7	7, 7, 8, 5, 5, 8	6, 1, 6, 4, 2, 8
2, 5, 5, 3, 9, 4	4, 8, 2, 1, 6, 3	1, 7, 8, 3, 5, 1	6, 3, 1, 4, 1, 8
1, 3, 1, 5, 8, 2	2, 9, 5, 5, 6, 3	4, 8, 4, 2, 4, 1	9, 5, 4, 9, 3, 1
4, 5, 7, 5, 2, 7	9, 5, 9, 3, 8, 8	1, 7, 2, 1, 6, 4	9, 4, 9, 2, 8, 9
6, 7, 9, 6, 6, 5	6, 3, 6, 3, 5, 2	2, 1, 3, 1, 6, 7	8, 7, 5, 4, 9, 2
2, 1, 5, 7, 1, 6	9, 6, 6, 2, 7, 6	2, 6, 2, 1, 5, 7	4, 6, 8, 8, 3, 3
6, 3, 3, 9, 4, 9	7, 5, 8, 8, 1, 8	2, 2, 3, 6, 5, 6	5, 8, 1, 1, 2, 7
5, 4, 8, 7, 1, 2	1, 2, 6, 8, 2, 9	8, 7, 2, 2, 7, 5	7, 3, 9, 1, 9, 6
6, 5, 8, 2, 5, 5	7, 8, 9, 8, 7, 7	4, 9, 6, 7, 6, 9	6, 6, 9, 7, 9, 4

Page 20	Page 23	Page 26	Page 29
2, 3, 3, 8, 4, 9	9, 5, 2, 2, 4, 3	7, 4, 2, 5, 4, 8	4, 9, 6, 1, 8, 3
4, 4, 6, 4, 9, 1	4, 3, 1, 5, 9, 3	9, 9, 3, 2, 7, 9	2, 9, 5, 7, 8, 2
4, 8, 2, 1, 9, 2	4, 8, 6, 6, 1, 6	4, 9, 7, 1, 5, 4	2, 5, 4, 2, 6, 9
3, 1, 6, 7, 5, 3	1, 8, 8, 9, 6, 3	6, 8, 5, 7, 6, 1	3, 2, 6, 5, 2, 4
4, 9, 2, 5, 8, 7	6, 7, 3, 8, 6, 2	3, 5, 5, 1, 8, 4	7, 4, 2, 4, 3, 9
5, 7, 1, 7, 3, 9	8, 5, 3, 2, 6, 1	4, 2, 3, 5, 2, 2	1, 7, 9, 2, 7, 8
5, 5, 6, 2, 3, 4	1, 1, 4, 2, 9, 4	4, 9, 6, 3, 9, 6	7, 2, 3, 7, 5, 8
1, 9, 5, 8, 9, 9	3, 2, 3, 4, 4, 5	1, 7, 4, 9, 1, 9	2, 7, 5, 8, 2, 4
1, 3, 8, 9, 5, 5	6, 5, 7, 5, 5, 9	3, 3, 5, 1, 5, 7	2, 6, 9, 9, 7, 3
8, 4, 6, 6, 9, 2	4, 5, 6, 6, 2, 1	3, 2, 3, 8, 3, 3	4, 7, 3, 3, 4, 9
9, 6, 2, 1, 7, 1	3, 8, 2, 3, 8, 1	5, 9, 7, 4, 3, 7	4, 6, 6, 8, 2, 4
2, 4, 6, 6, 8, 8	7, 5, 2, 9, 5, 9	6, 5, 4, 6, 5, 8	5, 7, 5, 7, 6, 7
Page 21	Page 24	Page 27	Page 30
9, 5, 3, 2, 2, 3	3, 4, 5, 7, 4, 4	2, 3, 5, 1, 8, 6	4, 8, 2, 8, 4, 5
6, 4, 2, 9, 6, 7	7, 8, 6, 2, 2, 9	7, 3, 7, 4, 4, 9	3, 7, 7, 8, 5, 6
7, 3, 3, 7, 4, 6	2, 5, 5, 5, 7, 4	9, 7, 8, 8, 5, 5	6, 7, 8, 2, 2, 4
5, 5, 5, 4, 2, 9	7, 7, 1, 4, 5, 8	8, 9, 8, 1, 1, 3	7, 4, 8, 7, 2, 4
1, 9, 7, 9, 6, 9	1, 8, 4, 8, 2, 8	5, 8, 1, 8, 3, 6	2, 4, 2, 7, 4, 3
3, 6, 6, 8, 4, 9	7, 5, 4, 9, 6, 5	3, 8, 3, 9, 9, 1	8, 9, 8, 9, 1, 9
4, 7, 4, 2, 6, 7	9, 5, 1, 9, 5, 1	1, 6, 5, 8, 5, 2	3, 8, 5, 5, 4, 2
8, 5, 3, 9, 1, 7	3, 8, 6, 4, 3, 6	5, 6, 5, 2, 7, 3	2, 7, 9, 4, 5, 5
7, 7, 4, 2, 5, 7	7, 1, 1, 5, 6, 2	6, 1, 2, 7, 6, 2	7, 3, 3, 8, 1, 6
3, 3, 1, 2, 1, 9	1, 1, 3, 4, 5, 8	2, 8, 3, 9, 9, 3	7, 3, 2, 8, 9, 4
8, 2, 6, 2, 5, 4	5, 7, 9, 6, 3, 2	3, 7, 3, 2, 4, 5	2, 3, 5, 4, 1, 5
2, 9, 5, 4, 5, 2	7, 6, 7, 2, 9, 2	9, 6, 3, 4, 9, 4	9, 5, 8, 7, 5, 9
Page 22	Page 25	Page 28	Page 31
4, 9, 8, 4, 4, 8	8, 3, 1, 5, 2, 1	3, 4, 8, 4, 9, 3	4, 2, 9, 5, 1, 4
3, 6, 3, 2, 9, 4	8, 5, 8, 5, 7, 2	7, 6, 9, 9, 3, 9	7, 3, 1, 7, 2, 9
9, 9, 4, 6, 6, 3	4, 7, 6, 9, 3, 8	6, 3, 7, 8, 7, 5	6, 5, 1, 4, 1, 3
3, 6, 5, 5, 2, 7	9, 2, 3, 9, 9, 6	9, 5, 5, 7, 4, 9	6, 2, 6, 8, 8, 4
9, 2, 2, 1, 8, 1	9, 3, 9, 8, 3, 8	2, 7, 4, 6, 3, 8	2, 5, 2, 3, 5, 9
8, 9, 4, 9, 8, 6	6, 9, 6, 1, 3, 2	4, 6, 8, 6, 4, 6	3, 3, 8, 7, 6, 3
5, 7, 6, 6, 6, 5	3, 7, 4, 5, 1, 1	9, 7, 5, 6, 3, 6	7, 9, 2, 9, 6, 2
9, 8, 2, 9, 3, 2	4, 1, 9, 3, 1, 5	1, 5, 2, 4, 1, 8	3, 9, 5, 9, 7, 4
9, 1, 7, 4, 8, 7	1, 1, 6, 8, 2, 7	1, 9, 3, 6, 3, 6	1, 9, 9, 5, 6, 3
8, 2, 7, 5, 8, 5	4, 5, 9, 5, 1, 6	5, 2, 9, 7, 9, 7	3, 6, 2, 7, 6, 4
4, 1, 6, 8, 7, 4	6, 1, 4, 2, 9, 8	3, 6, 5, 8, 2, 9	9, 3, 3, 7, 1, 7
6, 6, 3, 5, 5, 4	9, 9, 1, 1, 9, 1	3, 6, 2, 8, 6, 5	4, 4, 7, 4, 1, 9

Master Long Division with Remainders Practice Workbook

Part 2 Answers

Page 33
36, 56, 234, 10, 182
311, 10, 27, 122, 42
404, 456, 555, 61, 12

Page 34
54, 501, 19, 436, 264
74, 74, 487, 70, 455
874, 653, 909, 92, 96

Page 35
958, 32, 233, 237, 293
742, 478, 328, 733, 95
36, 858, 42, 900, 10

Page 36
66, 89, 181, 69, 181
88, 77, 63, 42, 684
707, 441, 186, 649, 12

Page 37
371, 147, 81, 46, 492
43, 403, 317, 114, 20
86, 14, 284, 796, 29

Page 38
97, 68, 79, 52, 95
663, 764, 36, 715, 77
35, 15, 32, 11, 82

Page 39
972, 896, 710, 60, 68
694, 96, 827, 447, 174
86, 42, 211, 47, 39

Page 40
16, 472, 712, 28, 965
85, 530, 47, 447, 829
29, 96, 413, 305, 12

Page 41
990, 190, 49, 77, 132
26, 939, 370, 50, 757
969, 944, 14, 26, 179

Page 42
45, 374, 43, 242, 89
756, 121, 231, 41, 27
879, 648, 620, 48, 966

Page 43
48, 775, 940, 110, 33
982, 179, 587, 67, 45
190, 159, 56, 75, 98

Page 44
76, 99, 985, 62, 569
78, 625, 896, 248, 620
237, 41, 85, 873, 957

Page 45
53, 96, 851, 96, 64
83, 20, 59, 793, 97
95, 429, 175, 74, 67

Page 46
126, 56, 594, 566, 181
116, 43, 22, 318, 84
795, 34, 31, 567, 969

Page 47
525, 374, 97, 778, 379
222, 37, 664, 452, 60
601, 699, 34, 250, 29

Page 48
73, 958, 79, 610, 860
818, 802, 98, 27, 103
172, 91, 47, 37, 68

Page 49
29, 22, 70, 591, 31
12, 56, 507, 36, 444
75, 944, 651, 295, 281

Page 50
35, 385, 746, 900, 556
118, 419, 68, 68, 636
48, 639, 761, 986, 711

Page 51
512, 246, 946, 24, 726
88, 88, 200, 57, 88
866, 471, 128, 642, 37

Page 52
118, 797, 92, 361, 76
153, 92, 735, 391, 50
898, 44, 529, 11, 421

Page 53
14, 144, 681, 764, 273
45, 438, 788, 88, 297
307, 973, 310, 97, 61

Page 54
289, 60, 141, 57, 572
357, 87, 195, 468, 950
255, 46, 213, 16, 70

Page 55
42, 79, 502, 99, 68
435, 99, 92, 38, 225
76, 90, 864, 799, 70

Page 56
381, 59, 81, 618, 42
42, 35, 203, 98, 34
220, 194, 90, 879, 93

Part 3 Answers

Page 58
88, 182, 47, 97
657, 342, 14, 620
790, 39, 60, 39

Page 59
79, 76, 27, 55
233, 89, 71, 496
98, 84, 726, 15

Page 60
360, 122, 810, 558
84, 427, 124, 52
92, 514, 488, 84

Page 61
11, 42, 538, 595
55, 662, 12, 624
500, 62, 414, 85

Page 62
867, 70, 678, 392
265, 15, 89, 58
618, 795, 72, 72

Page 63
58, 896, 97, 966
13, 503, 11, 242
33, 33, 82, 55

Page 64
474, 135, 78, 36
827, 189, 96, 915
920, 653, 17, 58

Page 65
446, 10, 61, 16
930, 857, 59, 95
209, 450, 67, 691

Page 66
428, 632, 785, 71
771, 617, 90, 58
87, 978, 99, 175

Page 67
46, 562, 709, 47
85, 740, 882, 335
33, 584, 149, 927

Page 68
649, 23, 14, 719
92, 66, 804, 367
23, 603, 319, 80

Page 69
912, 749, 16, 25
36, 258, 501, 48
987, 51, 255, 869

Page 70
213, 86, 684, 85
302, 82, 288, 963
709, 85, 12, 64

Page 71
210, 343, 945, 25
83, 735, 61, 58
370, 33, 384, 49

Page 72
83, 28, 544, 758
234, 82, 803, 30
45, 68, 74, 56

Page 73
986, 10, 69, 793
13, 59, 270, 70
961, 721, 24, 214

Page 74
13, 453, 298, 928
78, 34, 62, 12
381, 395, 802, 248

Page 75
319, 26, 507, 234
692, 160, 66, 70
15, 999, 435, 30

Page 76
226, 79, 431, 20
85, 197, 58, 96
530, 81, 88, 43

Page 77
10, 776, 132, 642
693, 61, 202, 734
522, 85, 731, 65

Page 78
70, 64, 14, 83
23, 728, 77, 521
340, 23, 318, 43

Page 79
89, 85, 934, 59
569, 152, 44, 12
880, 57, 206, 489

Page 80
58, 166, 72, 52
55, 165, 98, 889
412, 48, 97, 783

Page 81
47, 478, 86, 843
146, 316, 739, 83
970, 152, 304, 34

Master Long Division with Remainders Practice Workbook

Part 4 Answers

Page 83
4R1, 4R5, 9R2, 6R1, 5R3, 9R3
4R5, 2R5, 2R2, 8R6, 7R2, 9R1
7R1, 3R1, 7R3, 2R5, 7R2, 3R6
6R3, 6R3, 6R6, 9R1, 8R1, 7R1
6R3, 8R7, 6R7, 8R7, 4R1, 3R4
8R6, 8R5, 7R2, 4R1, 4R1, 6R1
4R4, 9R1, 7R1, 2R3, 5R1, 4R3
5R1, 6R8, 4R4, 6R1, 9R2, 3R3
5R1, 4R4, 6R5, 3R2, 3R1, 2R4
4R7, 4R4, 9R3, 9R1, 2R2, 7R1
3R2, 7R1, 3R5, 9R1, 4R4, 6R1
9R3, 8R1, 2R3, 3R3, 7R4, 5R6

Page 84
2R4, 8R2, 2R1, 6R7, 5R1, 7R3
9R2, 9R2, 6R1, 2R2, 9R1, 2R6
3R3, 8R2, 4R3, 7R4, 2R4, 7R3
3R2, 9R3, 5R3, 4R7, 2R1, 5R4
5R5, 4R1, 4R8, 2R1, 7R7, 8R4
5R2, 8R2, 2R1, 9R2, 2R2, 5R4
6R2, 5R3, 8R1, 5R5, 2R2, 7R1
4R2, 2R7, 2R8, 5R1, 9R3, 6R3
7R4, 4R4, 2R2, 5R2, 4R5, 6R1
8R1, 3R5, 8R1, 8R1, 9R5, 4R4
9R1, 8R2, 9R2, 7R1, 3R2, 4R1
2R4, 7R2, 4R1, 7R1, 2R7, 2R1

Page 85
4R1, 9R1, 5R1, 5R3, 6R1, 3R1
5R2, 2R3, 5R2, 8R1, 6R1, 7R4
6R1, 4R2, 3R6, 8R1, 2R1, 7R2
5R6, 4R2, 2R1, 9R2, 7R3, 8R2
9R5, 7R1, 2R2, 2R4, 4R1, 9R1
6R2, 6R2, 4R8, 6R6, 2R7, 2R4
4R1, 6R4, 6R3, 5R2, 7R5, 4R4
4R5, 8R1, 8R3, 8R4, 3R5, 6R4
4R1, 3R1, 7R3, 2R4, 6R1, 5R1
9R6, 9R2, 9R2, 7R5, 3R4, 2R5
4R5, 5R1, 3R2, 8R2, 3R8, 6R1
8R1, 4R3, 3R1, 8R2, 5R2, 6R6

Page 86
2R2, 8R1, 3R1, 4R1, 7R1, 9R6
2R1, 3R7, 6R4, 9R1, 2R5, 7R5
7R2, 5R4, 8R1, 8R2, 6R1, 4R2
3R1, 6R1, 5R4, 7R1, 6R2, 6R1
5R3, 2R8, 3R2, 7R3, 5R1, 2R2
2R5, 3R5, 4R4, 7R1, 2R1, 2R2
9R1, 5R2, 9R7, 9R1, 9R5, 4R6
2R6, 5R2, 2R8, 3R6, 8R1, 5R6
3R7, 7R1, 4R4, 3R2, 3R3, 2R5
3R2, 9R3, 4R7, 3R3, 8R3, 9R1
9R2, 2R5, 6R1, 3R1, 5R1, 4R3
9R2, 7R1, 9R1, 2R1, 9R1, 6R1

Page 87
3R2, 9R5, 4R5, 2R3, 3R2, 9R2
5R5, 3R4, 7R2, 4R1, 9R1, 7R6
5R4, 8R4, 9R1, 7R3, 4R1, 2R1
9R1, 2R2, 9R3, 5R2, 6R6, 5R1
4R1, 6R2, 5R4, 5R4, 8R1, 8R1
2R3, 7R1, 9R1, 4R5, 8R2, 9R2
8R1, 9R1, 4R3, 2R1, 6R4, 8R2
3R6, 4R1, 7R6, 7R1, 6R5, 6R6
9R1, 4R1, 9R1, 8R3, 7R3, 5R2
8R2, 2R6, 3R2, 9R2, 5R1, 6R1
7R1, 9R5, 8R4, 6R1, 9R1, 2R4
5R2, 4R1, 7R1, 2R2, 5R2, 5R1

Page 88
5R4, 8R2, 3R1, 9R3, 9R1, 9R4
9R3, 9R2, 6R1, 9R4, 2R1, 2R4
8R1, 2R6, 4R6, 5R6, 5R3, 9R1
3R3, 2R2, 7R3, 9R1, 2R2, 2R2
6R3, 5R1, 2R3, 2R2, 8R1, 2R4
9R2, 8R1, 2R1, 4R1, 2R2, 2R7
7R3, 2R3, 5R2, 7R5, 2R2, 5R5
7R2, 8R3, 7R3, 4R1, 7R3, 8R2
4R6, 4R2, 9R6, 8R1, 7R3, 8R2
6R8, 8R1, 2R1, 3R1, 6R6, 6R2
5R6, 6R3, 6R4, 9R2, 6R2, 5R5
2R5, 2R2, 5R3, 2R6, 8R3, 8R3

Page 89
5R8, 9R2, 4R6, 8R1, 6R2, 8R1
9R3, 3R3, 8R2, 6R1, 5R3, 8R5
2R2, 2R2, 6R6, 3R6, 9R6, 4R2
9R2, 7R1, 5R2, 4R5, 9R6, 4R4
9R2, 8R3, 2R5, 4R2, 3R4, 8R1
4R3, 2R5, 3R3, 4R4, 2R1, 7R2
3R1, 8R4, 7R4, 8R4, 7R1, 7R1
7R6, 9R3, 2R2, 6R1, 6R1, 4R4
5R4, 6R1, 4R4, 3R5, 4R1, 6R3
9R2, 4R1, 7R2, 8R1, 9R3, 3R3
7R6, 9R2, 3R2, 3R2, 4R2, 9R3
6R2, 6R7, 9R1, 9R1, 6R3, 4R2

Page 90
3R1, 2R5, 6R4, 4R5, 9R6, 9R1
2R4, 4R1, 7R1, 2R3, 9R1, 6R1
9R1, 9R4, 2R1, 7R1, 6R1, 2R5
7R5, 9R3, 7R3, 2R2, 2R2, 2R4
2R1, 9R2, 9R3, 6R1, 6R3, 2R4
5R3, 5R5, 6R2, 6R4, 3R2, 4R3
5R4, 7R1, 4R3, 5R2, 5R2, 9R1
5R4, 4R1, 4R1, 9R1, 3R1, 5R1
8R1, 4R4, 3R1, 8R4, 5R4, 2R2
4R2, 8R2, 7R1, 2R1, 6R2, 8R1
2R1, 5R1, 9R2, 4R1, 2R7, 3R1
6R4, 8R2, 4R5, 4R5, 8R6, 6R1

Page 91
6R2, 9R4, 3R7, 6R1, 6R3, 2R1
4R2, 4R3, 4R5, 4R1, 2R2, 3R5
9R1, 9R2, 8R1, 6R6, 6R1, 4R1
5R3, 4R4, 5R3, 4R6, 5R2, 5R2
6R1, 3R3, 9R1, 3R1, 5R2, 8R2
6R5, 2R2, 6R1, 6R4, 5R3, 6R4
9R4, 5R5, 4R1, 2R4, 5R4, 5R6
9R1, 8R3, 9R2, 8R3, 8R2, 3R6
4R6, 5R3, 6R5, 4R7, 6R1, 8R1
5R1, 9R1, 9R1, 3R2, 3R4, 6R1
6R1, 5R3, 7R4, 9R1, 3R1, 9R2
7R4, 7R2, 4R1, 8R4, 7R6, 4R1

Page 92
6R2, 5R4, 8R2, 8R1, 3R2, 5R4
8R2, 8R1, 7R1, 3R1, 3R2, 9R1
6R2, 9R1, 4R5, 5R2, 7R2, 4R1
7R8, 4R2, 9R4, 4R3, 6R1, 4R3
8R8, 9R3, 7R2, 4R7, 5R3, 6R1
6R2, 9R1, 7R5, 9R1, 5R2, 3R5
3R8, 3R1, 3R7, 5R5, 9R2, 9R6
3R1, 9R2, 5R1, 3R1, 3R3, 4R2
8R2, 4R6, 9R1, 2R2, 4R1, 2R1
3R1, 2R3, 3R3, 2R1, 8R6, 9R5
3R1, 7R2, 8R2, 2R1, 6R1, 4R1
2R4, 2R1, 2R4, 9R1, 6R2, 3R5

Page 93
9R1, 3R1, 6R3, 2R2, 9R3, 6R1
6R7, 8R1, 6R2, 8R2, 5R1, 5R1
8R5, 3R2, 9R3, 6R5, 6R6, 6R1
9R4, 4R1, 6R4, 6R4, 5R1, 7R2
9R2, 2R1, 2R3, 5R4, 7R1, 4R2
8R1, 9R4, 9R2, 6R3, 8R4, 9R8
5R3, 3R1, 4R4, 3R1, 5R1, 4R3
5R1, 4R4, 6R2, 6R7, 4R1, 6R3
7R3, 6R2, 5R6, 2R5, 4R2, 8R2
2R2, 2R3, 7R3, 9R2, 6R1, 2R2
7R3, 2R3, 8R1, 2R2, 5R2, 9R1
6R1, 4R2, 4R6, 6R1, 7R4, 4R1

Page 94
3R5, 3R4, 8R6, 5R1, 5R8, 6R7
8R8, 3R2, 9R4, 9R1, 7R2, 3R5
5R2, 4R4, 2R2, 6R1, 9R1, 9R2
5R1, 8R1, 8R1, 3R2, 3R1, 6R1
4R3, 7R5, 9R6, 5R1, 8R4, 4R3
2R1, 3R4, 2R1, 3R1, 5R5, 7R2
8R1, 3R4, 3R1, 7R3, 8R2, 7R2
9R5, 7R3, 5R8, 7R3, 2R1, 2R2
7R1, 2R2, 7R6, 6R2, 9R2, 4R5
9R3, 4R4, 4R2, 5R2, 7R5, 9R1
8R2, 6R5, 2R3, 2R3, 4R4, 4R3
8R2, 7R7, 7R1, 7R2, 3R1, 3R1

Page 95
2R5, 2R2, 8R3, 3R1, 2R3, 6R3
8R1, 5R5, 2R6, 3R1, 8R1, 3R3
3R1, 7R5, 8R2, 9R2, 3R1, 8R2
6R3, 6R7, 2R1, 5R1, 6R1, 7R5
7R3, 2R4, 4R4, 8R2, 4R5, 2R2
6R2, 3R1, 9R1, 7R1, 4R1, 8R3
9R2, 7R2, 6R1, 9R8, 4R1, 7R1
5R1, 6R1, 4R2, 6R2, 7R4, 9R2
8R1, 6R1, 6R1, 8R4, 9R1, 4R7
7R1, 5R1, 6R1, 4R2, 2R1, 3R1
7R2, 5R5, 6R4, 6R5, 4R8, 9R3
2R3, 6R7, 8R1, 5R2, 7R5, 2R1

Page 96
5R3, 4R1, 5R1, 5R2, 8R3, 6R3
8R3, 5R1, 3R1, 8R5, 3R5, 9R7
8R4, 3R1, 8R4, 2R1, 9R1, 9R4
8R2, 2R5, 8R1, 4R1, 4R2, 4R3
3R1, 6R8, 4R1, 8R1, 9R4, 7R4
3R2, 5R3, 5R3, 6R1, 5R6, 5R2
2R1, 2R6, 4R3, 3R5, 2R4, 7R1
2R2, 9R1, 3R3, 7R3, 2R3, 9R2
2R1, 7R2, 5R2, 3R3, 4R1, 6R1
5R8, 6R1, 8R3, 6R1, 7R4, 7R2
3R1, 5R1, 8R2, 5R4, 4R1, 4R3
9R3, 6R6, 8R1, 4R1, 4R2, 5R1

Page 97
2R2, 3R2, 7R5, 4R1, 3R2, 5R4
4R4, 5R3, 5R3, 9R2, 4R3, 7R3
4R2, 5R3, 4R2, 7R6, 6R3, 8R1
6R4, 4R1, 9R3, 7R3, 4R1, 2R1
9R6, 7R1, 3R3, 2R7, 7R1, 7R7
7R4, 3R6, 9R1, 4R1, 4R2, 6R4
7R1, 5R5, 6R1, 7R1, 3R7, 5R4
6R7, 3R1, 3R4, 6R1, 3R3, 9R1
6R3, 9R1, 4R5, 3R1, 9R4, 2R1
2R6, 9R1, 2R4, 3R6, 6R1, 3R1
6R5, 2R7, 6R2, 4R3, 9R6, 3R1
7R8, 8R5, 5R1, 6R7, 2R6, 2R4

Page 98
4R1, 9R1, 9R2, 8R1, 5R3, 3R1
7R2, 6R1, 7R1, 8R7, 2R7, 9R2
7R3, 7R2, 8R3, 6R7, 9R1, 6R1
3R2, 3R1, 2R1, 5R1, 2R1, 6R4
6R1, 7R3, 4R1, 8R1, 9R5, 3R3
6R2, 3R2, 4R3, 5R2, 4R1, 6R1
4R2, 4R2, 3R2, 6R1, 8R1, 2R2
5R7, 9R2, 9R1, 5R2, 5R6, 6R3
7R1, 7R1, 2R1, 9R1, 9R2, 9R2
6R3, 6R2, 2R1, 5R3, 5R3, 2R4
9R2, 5R4, 9R4, 3R3, 3R4, 4R1
3R7, 8R3, 5R6, 6R1, 8R7, 2R4

Page 99
5R2, 2R2, 6R1, 6R8, 9R1, 9R4
4R1, 6R3, 3R1, 7R1, 7R8, 9R4
2R3, 5R1, 2R1, 4R2, 8R3, 6R4
2R1, 9R1, 2R5, 2R4, 8R1, 7R2
2R4, 2R1, 6R4, 4R2, 2R3, 9R2
9R3, 9R2, 5R4, 7R6, 5R1, 6R1
5R2, 6R2, 2R1, 4R1, 8R6, 6R1
2R1, 6R4, 3R2, 9R3, 7R1, 7R5
2R1, 2R3, 7R5, 3R4, 7R2, 8R1
7R1, 2R4, 9R4, 9R5, 8R3, 9R3
3R3, 8R2, 8R2, 3R3, 9R1, 2R7
4R1, 5R3, 9R3, 4R1, 9R6, 2R1

Page 100
7R4, 8R3, 9R6, 5R2, 6R2, 7R1
8R2, 5R1, 5R6, 2R3, 3R1, 6R4
3R7, 6R2, 3R2, 7R1, 8R1, 5R2
5R1, 6R2, 4R1, 2R1, 3R1, 2R2
4R4, 4R2, 9R4, 7R7, 9R2, 9R3
7R4, 8R3, 6R6, 7R2, 8R4, 4R4
2R2, 2R8, 8R1, 6R5, 6R1, 7R1
4R2, 4R8, 3R3, 8R1, 7R1, 7R3
6R2, 8R3, 7R3, 3R5, 8R1, 8R2
6R2, 8R5, 7R7, 7R2, 2R2, 7R1
5R5, 9R1, 7R2, 5R3, 6R8, 5R1
8R1, 9R3, 7R3, 2R3, 8R3, 4R1

Page 101
8R5, 8R5, 6R1, 3R1, 3R1, 6R1
9R7, 4R4, 8R1, 8R5, 3R6, 5R5
2R6, 5R5, 8R1, 7R3, 3R3, 5R4
4R3, 6R2, 2R2, 3R2, 4R3, 3R1
2R1, 2R2, 5R1, 6R1, 7R1, 2R3
4R2, 4R1, 6R4, 6R7, 9R3, 5R1
8R1, 7R4, 4R2, 5R4, 6R5, 6R1
5R1, 8R5, 7R2, 5R2, 4R1, 9R1
9R4, 4R2, 9R4, 2R3, 3R4, 8R1
6R3, 2R4, 6R1, 7R1, 9R1, 6R7
4R2, 9R3, 2R3, 4R4, 4R1, 3R3
9R1, 4R2, 3R8, 8R1, 3R3, 5R2

Page 102
9R1, 7R5, 8R5, 6R6, 9R5, 6R1
5R1, 8R3, 8R7, 9R3, 4R4, 5R2
8R2, 8R4, 4R4, 2R5, 2R4, 6R2
8R6, 7R2, 6R4, 6R1, 5R2, 7R1
7R1, 4R1, 9R8, 9R7, 2R1, 8R2
2R4, 3R3, 8R3, 9R4, 6R2, 4R6
3R2, 6R2, 3R5, 8R2, 7R2, 5R4
4R3, 3R3, 3R5, 3R1, 9R2, 5R2
2R6, 7R1, 4R1, 7R1, 7R4, 8R3
7R7, 8R3, 8R3, 5R2, 4R3, 5R2
9R1, 4R2, 9R7, 9R6, 7R2, 2R4
2R2, 8R7, 3R2, 5R1, 2R2, 9R4

Page 103
4R4, 7R1, 3R2, 9R2, 2R7, 5R4
7R1, 9R6, 9R3, 6R3, 2R1, 5R1
5R3, 3R5, 7R2, 6R1, 6R1, 5R3
3R2, 5R7, 3R6, 9R1, 8R2, 7R2
5R2, 4R1, 6R4, 3R4, 6R3, 9R4
5R2, 8R2, 8R1, 2R4, 2R1, 4R1
8R2, 4R1, 4R1, 9R1, 8R2, 3R1
3R4, 6R5, 6R2, 5R2, 4R3, 7R6
9R7, 6R7, 3R1, 5R3, 9R2, 7R1
5R4, 8R2, 4R1, 8R5, 3R2, 6R1
5R5, 8R5, 7R2, 3R3, 2R1, 3R1
6R2, 9R4, 9R2, 9R1, 6R1, 4R6

Page 104
8R2, 6R1, 5R2, 2R6, 7R1, 5R5
7R2, 2R1, 9R1, 5R2, 4R2, 8R3
4R2, 7R1, 9R1, 9R2, 5R1, 4R2
7R5, 7R3, 3R5, 4R8, 7R3, 9R2
5R1, 4R1, 7R5, 5R1, 5R4, 8R1
5R5, 8R4, 9R2, 8R1, 5R3, 2R5
7R1, 6R2, 9R2, 5R4, 7R5, 9R1
7R1, 3R1, 3R1, 8R5, 2R2, 4R3
9R4, 6R1, 7R2, 5R4, 7R7, 2R2
7R6, 3R1, 2R3, 2R4, 8R2, 4R1
8R2, 5R2, 9R2, 4R2, 8R6, 7R4
5R1, 6R3, 3R1, 2R6, 6R5, 5R3

Page 105
9R5, 8R6, 7R2, 3R2, 9R2, 3R2
7R3, 9R2, 4R1, 7R4, 8R3, 3R5
5R1, 5R2, 3R2, 7R3, 7R2, 2R8
3R6, 8R1, 4R1, 5R2, 7R2, 3R7
2R2, 7R1, 5R4, 7R7, 3R3, 9R2
7R1, 2R2, 2R4, 4R2, 3R2, 6R5
2R3, 8R2, 4R1, 7R8, 2R1, 2R4
3R3, 2R1, 9R2, 6R2, 4R2, 7R4
7R3, 6R6, 4R7, 9R5, 6R2, 9R1
2R3, 8R3, 5R3, 6R5, 4R3, 8R1
8R3, 6R1, 5R4, 4R3, 9R3, 3R1
7R1, 3R1, 6R2, 5R2, 6R1, 7R2

Page 106
3R1, 5R1, 2R3, 6R1, 3R5, 2R1
4R2, 5R3, 7R1, 9R1, 6R3, 2R4
4R4, 6R3, 3R5, 4R7, 6R3, 3R1
6R1, 2R7, 9R1, 3R8, 8R2, 4R3
4R3, 9R2, 6R1, 7R1, 6R1, 2R1
6R3, 4R3, 5R6, 4R1, 7R1, 2R2
2R5, 6R2, 2R2, 3R2, 4R7, 5R4
3R2, 8R1, 8R2, 9R1, 3R1, 4R2
9R3, 3R2, 8R1, 9R4, 2R2, 2R2
7R4, 9R1, 5R8, 2R1, 7R1, 6R2
3R8, 2R1, 2R1, 9R5, 6R7, 3R1
5R2, 6R2, 4R3, 2R4, 4R1, 8R2

Part 5 Answers

Page 108
32R2, 94R4, 749R3, 60R3, 95R3
827R3, 97R2, 145R3, 599R2, 19R3
80R1, 284R2, 63R1, 33R3, 13R5

Page 109
183R1, 204R2, 87R1, 920R2, 881R3
10R4, 16R7, 804R4, 89R1, 616R1
13R1, 66R1, 949R5, 903R1, 505R2

Page 110
886R3, 291R6, 162R2, 410R4, 952R4
17R2, 68R1, 89R1, 967R2, 368R1
322R6, 41R5, 636R1, 347R2, 72R2

Page 111
88R4, 575R4, 852R6, 643R1, 321R6
768R2, 92R6, 82R3, 171R5, 87R3
684R1, 770R2, 65R4, 99R1, 18R5

Page 112
35R1, 146R4, 59R1, 928R1, 958R2
217R1, 84R2, 94R1, 997R1, 36R1
447R1, 56R6, 65R3, 36R4, 563R2

Page 113
879R1, 953R3, 75R2, 62R1, 396R2
71R1, 535R1, 523R1, 696R1, 71R5
296R2, 142R2, 69R3, 21R1, 96R2

Page 114
212R1, 771R1, 434R7, 560R4, 591R1
954R3, 17R5, 20R3, 76R1, 511R2
872R2, 593R3, 897R2, 33R5, 44R1

Page 115
466R1, 47R2, 793R2, 82R4, 44R4
906R1, 82R3, 755R6, 20R1, 97R1
91R1, 824R5, 22R1, 440R4, 492R2

Page 116
55R1, 76R2, 26R3, 352R5, 333R4
39R4, 35R2, 35R2, 65R1, 19R1
788R3, 379R1, 68R2, 897R2, 65R2

Page 117
74R2, 45R4, 27R4, 66R2, 80R2
961R2, 68R2, 95R5, 547R1, 41R6
452R1, 820R2, 480R8, 944R2, 37R3

Page 118
96R2, 48R3, 34R1, 22R1, 10R3
925R2, 33R4, 434R1, 233R4, 38R7
861R1, 16R3, 30R1, 46R3, 23R1

Page 119
49R1, 46R3, 572R3, 355R3, 90R4
126R2, 898R1, 21R2, 46R5, 71R1
703R4, 71R3, 55R3, 930R2, 885R3

Page 120
569R2, 301R1, 327R4, 916R5, 29R5
548R1, 389R3, 924R1, 37R2, 655R2
160R1, 449R1, 336R2, 49R1, 61R4

Page 121
845R1, 97R2, 969R2, 661R4, 71R2
24R3, 87R1, 62R2, 25R2, 336R2
17R2, 845R1, 97R1, 562R2, 638R2

Page 122
93R1, 84R1, 38R4, 34R1, 76R2
877R1, 461R8, 38R1, 11R4, 13R1
670R6, 495R4, 70R3, 526R3, 489R5

Page 123
35R5, 951R2, 226R1, 897R2, 358R1
88R1, 42R1, 337R3, 95R5, 53R4
495R4, 788R3, 78R2, 365R3, 297R1

Page 124
691R5, 10R6, 892R1, 48R3, 251R1
392R3, 52R1, 69R1, 476R4, 26R1
509R4, 928R2, 63R3, 498R2, 260R1

Page 125
97R1, 827R3, 898R3, 877R5, 58R2
99R2, 13R3, 43R1, 41R5, 15R5
72R5, 221R5, 34R3, 50R3, 37R1

Page 126
28R7, 400R3, 689R1, 50R4, 905R1
506R1, 21R8, 703R3, 27R4, 41R1
585R3, 179R2, 79R2, 627R1, 28R1

Page 127
664R3, 357R1, 64R2, 591R2, 20R3
94R5, 873R1, 559R4, 413R1, 10R5
60R3, 160R6, 55R1, 46R1, 10R8

Page 128
23R2, 465R3, 83R2, 840R1, 71R1
14R4, 194R1, 910R1, 913R2, 72R8
189R2, 505R2, 129R5, 75R1, 73R1
Page 129
640R5, 148R1, 546R3, 100R2, 43R7
774R2, 402R3, 806R3, 74R1, 737R4
166R2, 11R1, 988R3, 652R2, 59R7

Page 130
914R8, 382R6, 803R1, 887R2, 946R2
80R1, 13R2, 18R2, 23R2, 98R4
16R3, 32R2, 18R1, 31R1, 87R3
Page 131
504R1, 92R1, 48R5, 189R3, 80R3
68R1, 665R3, 86R1, 98R3, 64R1
515R1, 22R1, 925R1, 732R2, 761R6

Part 6 Answers

Page 133
75R7, 33R3, 91R8, 64R8
731R3, 77R9, 176R7, 129R4
234R1, 604R8, 15R4, 727R4
Page 134
65R9, 576R8, 190R1, 38R3
67R4, 689R2, 10R2, 23R7
260R2, 59R4, 26R9, 452R6
Page 135
984R5, 80R9, 18R5, 291R4
234R4, 68R3, 259R4, 903R6
13R9, 543R9, 258R6, 328R7
Page 136
773R6, 13R4, 656R6, 384R3
742R6, 865R4, 991R2, 62R3
978R9, 929R7, 77R3, 30R5
Page 137
18R4, 465R1, 483R3, 12R2
48R8, 656R2, 782R2, 303R6
633R1, 64R7, 78R9, 69R3
Page 138
149R6, 88R3, 90R3, 770R1
14R3, 670R9, 758R9, 84R6
813R8, 48R6, 55R9, 252R2
Page 139
645R1, 73R6, 67R3, 39R3
456R6, 58R4, 20R8, 978R7
228R6, 797R5, 428R7, 820R4
Page 140
641R1, 27R8, 47R2, 228R7
10R7, 532R6, 362R8, 317R3
732R4, 438R2, 84R5, 749R8

Page 141
16R5, 239R7, 34R9, 67R7
300R9, 580R8, 357R7, 90R4
16R8, 74R2, 94R7, 725R7
Page 142
365R1, 90R1, 922R3, 199R9
110R6, 747R8, 14R9, 255R7
43R4, 95R8, 10R5, 29R7
Page 143
43R2, 24R4, 183R7, 83R2
328R1, 874R6, 367R3, 455R3
936R2, 533R6, 68R3, 536R1
Page 144
867R2, 67R3, 43R3, 658R2
476R1, 580R9, 627R2, 527R9
46R2, 66R6, 44R2, 34R1
Page 145
37R9, 651R5, 557R2, 915R2
74R2, 541R3, 35R7, 98R2
691R3, 48R1, 568R7, 90R4
Page 146
64R4, 676R3, 13R1, 74R7
18R2, 68R6, 49R3, 55R4
614R6, 214R4, 89R2, 50R3
Page 147
150R6, 37R3, 353R9, 393R8
767R8, 84R9, 362R1, 710R4
912R3, 48R1, 17R3, 108R8
Page 148
13R5, 56R9, 741R3, 80R7
83R3, 253R1, 96R5, 126R6
702R1, 802R9, 948R6, 442R9

Page 149
346R3, 90R9, 716R8, 72R3
32R3, 908R4, 17R1, 39R5
97R1, 59R1, 82R8, 11R7

Page 150
451R9, 467R9, 79R9, 55R7
230R9, 672R4, 95R3, 640R6
10R6, 440R6, 991R5, 91R6

Page 151
31R7, 32R1, 39R5, 193R2
21R8, 909R4, 81R2, 56R3
360R1, 201R9, 62R1, 69R3

Page 152
929R7, 81R8, 30R8, 501R7
699R5, 69R2, 917R5, 69R5
72R2, 992R1, 458R3, 67R8

Page 153
634R4, 99R6, 76R7, 78R4
902R9, 210R9, 819R6, 274R7
67R4, 122R1, 194R4, 507R7

Page 154
81R3, 11R6, 585R2, 53R4
87R9, 91R6, 59R5, 687R5
27R2, 44R5, 73R7, 946R6

Page 155
440R3, 809R1, 76R4, 871R7
624R1, 473R6, 89R2, 760R2
74R3, 70R6, 46R4, 84R3

Page 156
740R8, 539R7, 795R9, 49R5
842R2, 189R9, 67R5, 28R2
823R3, 90R2, 11R8, 867R4

Made in the USA
Columbia, SC
05 December 2018